TELE SELLING

HIGH PERFORMANCE
BUSINESS•TO•BUSINESS
PHONE SELLING
TECHNIQUES

PHILLIP E.
MAHFOOD

IRWIN

ISBN 1-55738-500-9

Printed in the United States of America

BC

4 5 6 7 8 9 0

Dedication

This book is dedicated to my father. Long before computers printed out customers' names and buying habits, long before the telephone was an accepted mode of selling, long before I even thought about becoming a salesman, my dad was the best there was.

Contents

☾ *Phone Scenarios* ☾

Preface

In the last decade telemarketing has become a household word. And well it should be. There is virtually no product that cannot be sold over the telephone and, with the advent of the universal credit card and the Wide Area Telephone Service (WATS), the age of the telemarketer is here. Boiler rooms have given way to more sophisticated approaches, and those once considered "pitchmen" are now telemarketing specialists. In short, what was once the seedier side of selling has now become a respectable, even desirable profession.

It is the purpose of this book to unravel the mysteries of what makes one person succeed and another fail in the arena of telephone selling. There are really no secret rites involved in phone sales. There are no magic words, no clandestine formulas which are guarded by temple dogs and chanted only on nights with full moons. There are, however, certain guidelines which, when adhered to, will result in increased productivity, regardless of whether the products are toys, batteries, corporate stocks, brake shoes, or leather goods.

When I started in telemarketing fifteen years ago, few people had heard of it, and those that did had a negative connotation about phone sales. Since those days, I have set up numerous telemarketing operations, selling everything from electronics to auto parts, from cemetery plots to political contributions and circus tickets. I've taught continuing education in Florida as well as Texas and am currently the CEO of my own firm. Last year our company booked orders in excess of $1.9 million, each and every penny of which came over the phone lines. *We do not employ a single road man!*

Introduction

Selling over the telephone is to regular sales what riding an elephant is to walking a tightrope. Both are difficult, but both can be mastered with time and effort.

This book addresses two components of telemarketing. First, we will examine actual telephone strategies for the individual salesman. We will learn how his performance can be increased and his sales enhanced through illustration. Robert Jeffers, a phone solicitor working for the imaginary Selmore Corporation, will serve as our guide. We will join him in his day-to-day battle with the "enemy," learning from his successes as well as his setbacks.

I will also detail the actual mechanics of how a telemarketing program works in conjunction with other marketing and sales programs. Actual examples from selected industries will serve as models which, with very little effort, can be adapted to suit any business.

It is my intention to walk you through the day-to-day job as it is now done across the nation and in almost every industry. This book will show you how to begin the sale, how to talk to someone you've not spoken to before, how to put the customer at ease, and, most importantly, how to close the order.

If tomorrow I were to find myself in the heart of Manhattan or if I woke up in a small town in Kansas, I would not only be able to make a living, but a damn fine one at that. The reason? I know how to sell on the telephone. It doesn't matter what the product is, it doesn't matter how stiff the competition, I could sell it and sell it by the ton. So can you. Once you have mastered the basics, the products become virtually interchangeable.

There are few businesses in America that are not totally dependent on the efforts of their sales departments. As our economy continues to drift away from the traveling salesman and move more toward the telephone as the main source of income, telemarketing has become teleselling—a vital sales method used by corporate America.

There is more to telemarketing than merely picking up the phone and asking for an order. This book is laid out in such a manner that by the time the reader finishes the last chapter, he will be ready to tackle any sales challenge. Remember, there is no lack of opportunity in the field of telemarketing, only a lack of qualified practitioners.

one

Overcoming the Rudeness Factor Inherent in Telemarketing

It would be safe to say that not a person holding this book has gone through life without an intimate association with Mr. Bell's invention. From a baby in the crib and a girl sitting home alone on Friday night to an anxious father of the girl not sitting at home alone on Friday night—we all know the telephone, and we know it well. It is as familiar to us as junk mail and junk television. And, at times, no doubt, we view its use as junk calls.

But consider the magnitude of the instrument. Without a doubt the telephone is the rudest of man's creations. It is a respecter of neither privacy nor intimacy. It does not care what time of day it rings, nor what we might be doing when it does. It will ring as we bathe and as we sleep. It will summon us as we are on our knees proposing and will ring as we are confessing all to our closest friend.

Imagine what our reaction would be to any other such intrusion in our lives. With the rarest of exceptions, no one sits next to a phone waiting with breathless anticipation for it to ring. Almost anything we are doing—almost any activity in which we are engaged—is more important than answering the phone.

How then, can this instrument be considered a sales tool? Why is it used with such a high degree of success? The answers lie in the basic character of all people. We all want to be noticed. We all want to be recognized. We reach for the phone while watching TV, while eating lunch, and while reading. (But not right now! This book is too important to stop to answer the phone. They'll call back. Keep reading!)

Imagine Mr. Smith at work. A major project that has hovered over him, depriving him of a restful night, lies on his desk. His supervisor is standing in front of his desk, asking about his progress (or lack thereof) and Smith is desperately trying to explain that everything is under control, when—suddenly, literally out of nowhere—a person who was not there one second earlier jumps on his desk, pushes aside his project, steps between him and the boss, and starts talking without so much as an "excuse me"!

You have just conjured up a typical business phone call. Without missing a beat, Smith must handle the interruption and return to the exact spot he was when the call came in. What a task! Yet we all do it every single day, and somehow we survive without any noticeable injuries.

WHAT TO SAY IN THE FIRST FIFTEEN SECONDS

The hard fact is that from the time the caller hears the first word, "Hello," he has *fifteen seconds* to capture the attention of the recipient. In these fifteen seconds, the person who has been interrupted must decide if the call is important enough for him to divert his attention and place the call ahead of what he was doing. While not a lot of time, these fifteen seconds will set the scenario: in fifteen seconds a salesman can either alienate a prospective customer and send him running into the arms of a competitor or grab his attention and, hopefully, make a sale.

What to do in these fifteen seconds? Selling on the phone is very much like trying to make a date with a person you've just met. First impressions *are the only thing!* When trying to impress a member of the opposite sex, people often do so with superficial visual ploys such as looks or money. We might flex a muscle or bend over to tie our seventy-five dollar running shoes. We might allow our Rolex to slide down our wrist or pay for a purchase with our gold card. But on the phone it doesn't matter what shape we are in or how much magic plastic is in our billfold. All we have is our voice and our intelligence.

FINDING THE PERSON WHO CAN BUY

The first and most important step to a successful sales call is getting the right person on the phone. Make sure you are talking to a *buyer*. The best sales pitch in the world is useless if the person you are pitching to is not the decision maker.

If you do not know the buyer's name, there are ways to secure this information before getting him or her on the line. Whoever answers the phone will likely know who you are seeking. If they do not, they can direct you to someone who does. Again, be positive in your approach. *Ask:* "Who does the buying for your electronics department?" *Do Not Ask:* "May I speak to the buyer for the electronics department?" By asking who the buyer is, you've eliminated the need for a two-sided introduction on the phone.

✆   *TeleSell 1*   ✆
Learning the Buyer's Name (Part 1)

Ring . . . Ring . . . Ring.

"Kelley Department Store. May I direct your call?"
"Yeah. I want to speak to the buyer for electronics."
"Thank you, I'll ring."
Ring . . . Ring . . . Ring.
"Hello."
"Yes Ma'am, who am I speaking with?"
"Who did you want?"
"Well, I don't know—"

Click.

Instead, try:

✆   *TeleSell 2*   ✆
Learning the Buyer's Name (Part 2)

Ring . . . Ring . . . Ring.

"Kelley Department store. May I direct your call?"
"Thank you. Who is the buyer for your Electronics Department?"
"That would be Mr. Smith. Shall I connect you?"

"Please."

Ring . . . Ring . . . Ring

"Hello."

"Mr. Smith, please.

"Speaking."

The conversation will start at a more professional level; immediately you know the buyer's name. The worst that can happen is that you will be told Mr. Smith is the buyer, but is not in now. Sure, you've tipped your hand, but you can always call back. Next time, you'll not have to stop at the switchboard on your way to make the sale.

You now have the right person on the phone. Smith has answered your call, and now it's your move. What do you do next? What will you say in those fifteen seconds? Actually, *what* you say will not be nearly as important as *what you do not* say. Remember, you have only fifteen seconds to impress your prospective customer.

It is very important that you do not confuse manners with business practices. Do not burden yourself or your prospect with unnecessary politeness. In view of the fact that we are severely restricted in the amount of time we have to involve the prospect in our sales effort (fifteen seconds), it is imperative that the bulk of that time be used for the specified purpose of getting down to business. There is a time for manners and a time for business.

Imagine the aforementioned scenario with the harried buyer, his desk full of problems, his boss standing in front of him. The phone rings and he answers it:

ⓒ   TeleSell 3   ⓒ

How Not to Start the Conversation

Ring . . . Ring . . . Ring

"Hello."

"Mr. Smith, please."

"Speaking."

"Mr. Smith, you don't know me, but my name is Robert Jeffers. How are you today?"

"What?"

"I asked how you are today."

"Can I do something for you?"

"Well, actually, I wanted to talk to you about my company. I work for the Selmore Corporation. We're calling new prospective buyers and telling them a little about ourselves. Do you have a few minutes to talk to me?"

"Tell you what. Why don't you give me your number and I'll get back with you?"

What was wrong here? Robert was *too* polite. In his attempt to endear himself to Smith, he laid out enough manners to greet a queen, not a buyer. Both men knew that the purpose of the call was to sell a product. Both men knew they were strangers, and neither man really cared how the other was "doing" today, aside from the fact that Robert hoped Mr. Smith would be in a receptive mood.

But Robert tipped his hand. He actually asked a total stranger, "How are you today?" The first rule in successful business-to-business telemarketing is never ask a prospective new buyer how he is! You are wasting his time, you are insulting his intelligence, and worse, your initial presentation is weak. You allow yourself to sound like a person reading a script, a person who casts his line into the water hoping that some fish will bite. This sort of approach rarely works.

One of the first rules taught to all aspiring lawyers is: when examining a witness, never ask a question for which you don't already know the answer. This is as true for a phone salesman as for Perry Mason. The scenario could have gone wrong from the first sentence:

✪   TeleSell 4   ✪

The Horror Scenario

"Mr. Smith, please."

"Speaking."

"Mr. Smith, you don't know me, but my name is Robert Jeffers. How are you today?"

"Not so good, Bobby. May I call you Bobby? I just found a letter from my wife's boyfriend asking her to run away with him. My daughter's pregnant and can't remember the name of the rock group responsible. My son told me last night he thinks that he might be gay. My father fell and broke his hip this morning. He doesn't have insurance, which means my brother, the alcoholic, and my sister, the Zen Buddhist, will undoubtedly expect me to pay the entire bill myself. And the damn dog's got the mange. What can I do for you?"

Are you really going to ask this man to buy from your company? Or are you going to make some lame excuse about how this is probably not a good time to talk and tell him you will call back later? What happened here? The customer got the jump on Robert by using his pretense of concern—"How are you today?"—to shame him into hanging up the phone and not bothering him with some new product or company. You can be assured that as both men returned the headset to the cradle, Smith had a broad smile on his face, while Robert had only egg on his.

But if politeness is not effective, how do you get the prospect to talk to you? I didn't say you shouldn't be polite, I said don't get carried away. There is a difference between holding the door for a person carrying packages and summoning a skycap to carry his or her bags. One is common courtesy, the other is overstepping the bounds of business behavior.

The proper way to greet a new account, a prospective customer, is with courtesy and authority. Remember, you only have fifteen seconds to make this guy want to continue the conversation. Don't waste any of that precious time. Make each word count. Pick your words and your images carefully!

MAKING THE FIRST CONTACT

☎   TeleSell 5   ☎

Introducing Yourself

"Mr. Smith, please."

"Speaking."

"Mr. Smith, my name is Robert Jeffers. I'm with the Selmore Corporation. We sell a product you now use and have a plan to save you money and time. Our company is owned locally and can schedule deliveries to suit your needs. The savings to you will result in increased bottom-line profits. Let me explain . . ."

Do you see the difference? No, Robert didn't inquire as to the state of the buyer's health. But then, Robert is not a doctor, he is a salesman, and he did was what he is paid to do. He started selling the moment Smith was on the line. Let's break this introduction down into two parts:

1) *"My name is Robert Jeffers, and I'm with the Selmore Corporation."*

Robert identified both himself and his company in one sentence. It wasn't necessary to tell Mr. Smith that he didn't know him. Unless Smith is a complete idiot, he knows most of his acquaintances by name. In the first sentence, Robert took control of the conversation. He identified his prospect, he identified himself, and he identified the company for which he works.

2) *"We have a product that you are now using and have a plan to save you both money and time."*

The second sentence reinforced the image of Robert being a strong starter. In sales, strength denotes success and success indicates profit. Robert also points out that the product he sells is one Smith already buys. He doesn't need to return to college to learn what to do with Robert's new product. But, most importantly, Robert hit on the two most important aspects of Mr. Smith's professional life. Money and time! All this, plus a plan! A plan! This is the best phone call Smith has received in a week. A plan, more money, and saved time, all in one deal!

There are other key words and phrases here such as "locally owned" and "your needs." Phrases like "bottom-line profits" and "savings to you" are as welcome as a life raft on a leaky boat. Key words are what the first fifteen seconds are all about.

These key words are "triggers." They start the buyer's juices flowing. They are important words. The more you use trigger words, the longer the conversation. Your ability to make the sale is contingent on the buyer's continued interest in talking to you. You absolutely must make the buyer hungry to talk to you! He must have a desire to buy at least equal to your desire to sell. In order to induce his desire, you must seduce him with the words he will react to.

IN PARTING . . .

Most importantly, a good telemarketer never lies or misrepresents his product. For continued, profitable relationships, the telemarketer must have integrity. He must tell the truth. But truth is a coat of many colors. It is up to the salesman to romance his product, to make it truly desirable, to create a need for his product. So while we want to tell the buyer what he wants to hear, stick with the truth. A sale built on untruths or half-truths is likely to create more in problems than in profits.

two

The Application of Pricing as It Relates to the Telemarketer

Nothing can be assumed in phone sales. The telemarketer cannot assume the gender, race, political bias, or sexual preference of the buyer. We cannot assume, for example, that a buyer in charge of purchasing boxing gloves named "Rocky Granitello," who answers the phone with a "Yo?" is a fight enthusiast. The old adage, "If it walks like a duck, quacks like a duck, and swims like a duck, it probably *is* a duck," doesn't hold water in telephone sales. All you can be sure of is that this person is a buyer who may be persuaded to purchase a few gross of your company's fine product, "The Selmore Golden Boxing Glove."

Let's get Mr. Granitello on the telephone:

11

✆ *TeleSell 6* ✆

First Call to a New Prospect

Ring . . . Ring . . . Ring.

"Yo?"

"Mr. Granitello?"

"Speaking."

"My name is Robert Jeffers, and I'm with the Selmore Sporting Goods Company. We've developed a glove I feel that you might be interested in seeing. It has several advantages over the other gloves currently being marketed in this area; most notably, they are lighter, therefore easier to ship, and the packaging makes them more appealing to the ladies who shop in your store. In addition to this we have a special introductory offer which will save you additional dollars, as well as special extended terms. You do sell a good number of gloves, don't you?"

"Yeah, gloves are a major part of our sporting goods business, but right now I've already got a supplier who delivers to my door, gives me ninety days, and takes care of any defectives I have. How much are your standard gloves, say a size six?"

FINDING THE BUYER'S MOTIVATION

What we have here is a buyer who doth protest too much. He already has the ideal supplier. He gets free freight, he has great terms, and he has no hassles with warranty. Then why did he ask the price? In phone sales, you listen not only to what the buyer is saying, but also to what he is not saying. He praised his current supplier in three areas: delivery, terms, and warranty, *but not price.*

He is clearly not happy with the amount he pays for gloves from his current supplier. Thus, he is clearly a price-conscious buyer. Remember, not all clients are price-conscious (a dangerous assumption). If price were the only consideration or even the final consideration in all transactions, we would all be driving ten-year-old Chevys.

In this case, however, it is price that will grab Mr. Granitello's attention. Robert has a chance to score here and will if he can appeal to the buyer's sense of economy. But of even greater importance than the fact that Granitello is asking price is the fact that he is still on the phone.

Selling is like playing catch. Remember, as a kid you'd toss a ball to a pal, and he'd toss it back. This could go on for hours as long as both of you, upon receiving custody of the ball, would immediately toss it back to the other.

ESTABLISHING DIALOG

Telemarketing works exactly like a game of toss between two people.

You toss: "I have a product that I believe you will be interested in."

He tosses back: "What's your price on a standard glove, size six?"

You toss back: "Do you buy those in dozens or grosses?"

He returns: "Usually, we buy three dozen at a time."

Do you see what is happening here? Robert engaged his buyer in a meaningful discussion concerning the price of a specific product he handles. Robert has cleared the first three hurdles in the quest for the sale: (1) he identified and is talking to the right buyer; (2) he established himself as a person worth talking to; and (3) he snared the attention of the buyer.

However, long before Mr. Jeffers picked up his phone and placed a call to Mr. Granitello, he knew a good deal about his prospective client. He makes studies of buyers and classifies them all into one of three general categories.

THE THREE CATEGORIES OF BUYERS

The Visionary

The visionary buyer is a buyer who can, with a bit of help from the telemarketer, actually see the product being promoted as it would be displayed on the shelf of his store. He thinks of the product in terms of its display in the store; volume sales; and the eventual reorder. He can visualize the actual movement of the new product and can see his role as the prime mover and shaker of great merchandising concepts. He is, in short, half sold before Robert opens his mouth.

The visionary buyer must sell himself on the concept before you can sell him a product. He wants to fulfill his half of the contract; that is, he wants to buy. But, more importantly, he must be able to see himself selling that which he bought.

Visionary buyers think along the same lines whether they are buying charity tickets for a concert to benefit the homeless children or buying boxing gloves for a sporting goods store. Your objective is the same regardless of the product. You must help the buyer put your product to use. It is very important that you allow the visionary buyer to help you sell your product to him. He wants to be in on the kill. He wants to show you his foresight and his wisdom. Let him help.

The Emotional Buyer

The emotional buyer has to *feel* that the product is right. He is not as concerned with price as he is the product arriving at a time when it can best be promoted to its fullest capacity and therefore realize a larger market share of the total dollars available to be spent on this type of product.

If you are pitching a new product, a first-time service or an innovative concept, he must be convinced that what you are saying is true, not only on the superficial level of pricing and delivery, but also on the emotional level of need and fulfillment. The emotional buyer will buy out of a need to fulfill a deep emotional craving. He may have three dozen sets of gloves in inventory, all identical to the ones you are proposing he purchase. He may have bought them for the same price you are quoting. But you can sell him if you can appeal to an emotion such as fear, greed, or pride.

For instance, you can convince the emotional buyer that a shortage could occur, that a price increase is forthcoming, or that his competitors are better stocked. Pricing, delivery, and advertising issues will not make the sale with this type of buyer. Only by sensing his emotional needs will you break through and snag the order. Ignore his emotions and you can forget your commission.

The Analyzer

The analyzer is the buyer who must believe he needs the product right now before he will place an order. You cannot spin a story of great visions for this person, nor can you panic him into buying your product. You cannot appeal to him through any of the usual channels. To sell this buyer you must clearly demonstrate that his needs will be fulfilled by your product. Nothing else will do. His purchasing decisions are based on a computer-generated mentality. If he has six pairs of the standard size six glove in stock and has sold only two pairs in the last six months, he knows that his supply will last another eighteen months.

To sell this buyer you must show him, in detail, why there is about to be an upsurge in demand for your product. The broadcast of a hotly contested boxing match, the arrival of a new head coach to lead the local college to the top of the amateur boxing league, or the building of a new gym in his neighborhood are the types of reasons he might believe would warrant an increase in inventory levels. But to give vague and groundless concepts to a person of this persuasion is to waste your time and ultimately your money.

Robert sized up Mr. Granitello when he asked the price of Robert's gloves and seized the opportunity to make a sale. Granitello is not a visionary, he didn't see new horizons to be conquered with the Selmore Glove; he wasn't an emotional buyer, he didn't feel a need to buy more gloves in order to ward off a horde of panic buyers, who, in a buying frenzy, looked to him to supply their pugilistic needs. No, he wanted to know how much the gloves cost. He was prepared to analyze the cost factor and compare the savings to the benefits of continuing with his current supplier.

QUOTING A PRICE

Robert can close this sale, but not unless he first comes to realize where his strength lies. It does not lie with his company, nor with his product. In the case of Mr. Granitello, only lower prices will close this deal. Thus, he need lay out a cold economic fact without actual knowledge of what the competition is doing. He must quote the price! This is the most critical part of the phone conversation and the part where most sales are made or lost, not solely because the price may be higher than what the buyer is now paying, but because from this point on, the honeymoon is over. In the beginning, Granitello was willing to offer Robert the benefit of the doubt. Now, with the price on the table, all that remains is the actual decision of whether or not to favor Robert with the order. If he quotes a price lower than the competition, all other factors being equal, he may get an initial order. If he quotes a price equal to or higher than the competition, the game could be over. *But,* if he can romance the price, if he can make Granitello feel as if price is not the sole determining factor, he may well have found that elusive quarry—the buying buyer!

The function of the buyer is to buy. This may sound incredibly simple, but it is the essence of the industry. Along with his responsibility to buy, it is incumbent upon the buyer to make intelligent purchases. He must purchase goods with an eye toward demand, delivery, and profit. He must consider not only what is now selling well in his store, but also what will sell well next month and next season. Just as important, he must assess what will not sell and curb his inventory of that item before it becomes obvious he was not able to forecast a downtrend.

Buying is a particularly tricky job. A buyer can purchase $60 million worth of great products and make his company tons of profits. However, the successes are often immediately forgotten with one bad purchase that loses his company money. The hard, cold truth about buying is that every *good* deal the buyer makes is sold out quickly, the profits banked, and time goes on. Every *bad* deal he is associated with lingers in the storerooms and on the inventory sheets for month after month, quarter after quarter, until, at the annual meeting, the president of the company asks the dreaded question, "Who purchased sixty gross of snow shovels for the Miami store?"

To paraphrase Mark Antony's address to the Romans during Caesar's funeral, the good that buyers do is oft interred with them, the blunders live long after they are fired.

THE BUYER'S DILEMMA

It is, therefore, true that every buyer is faced with a two-sided problem. If he doesn't buy, there will be nothing to sell and his company will fire him. If he buys the wrong goods that do not sell, his company will fire him. He must seek a middle ground—buy that which will sell. With a little luck and a lot of experience, he hopes to remain on the cutting edge of his industry. Luck is for rabbits. Experience is just remembered history. What he keenly needs (and this is a scary thought to all buyers) is the assistance of sales representatives to help him do his job.

Mr. Granitello has, with the assistance of the people he currently buys from, built a wall around himself to help hold back the floodwaters of destruction that constantly await the relaxation of his vigil. It is this wall that keeps Robert from selling the gloves he needs to sell and that Mr. Granitello needs to buy. But, as with all old walls, there are cracks. In this case, the crack takes the form of pricing. However, it could as easily have been in the shape of delivery, terms, or warranty.

IN PARTING . . .

Remember, price is not the most important factor in every transaction. If price was the only consideration, we would all sleep in cheap motels and wear secondhand clothes. There *is* a correlation between cost and value received. Just as consumers spend money on that which is perceived to be of value, so too does the business buyer. Show the buyer he will receive value for his money, and make the sale. Failing to provide evidence of the product's value will result in no sales—now and down the line. There is a direct relationship in the quantity of sales and the telemarketer's level of astuteness.

three

Overcoming General Objections and Finding Acceptable Solutions

If it is true that as a salesman, Robert must sell, and as a buyer, Mr. Granitello must buy, then where lies the problem? It would seem that all Robert has to do is make his customer aware that the product is available and proceed to write the order. Right? *Wrong!* Nothing comes easy in this life, and that goes double for telemarketing. It is a good deal more complicated. With a microscopic examination of the process, Robert will learn and will hone his craft.

LISTENING TO WHAT THE BUYER IS SAYING

The primary reason any salesman, particularly a telemarketer, fails to secure an order is the failure to overcome an objection. Again, this sounds obvious. Be assured, it is not.

Salesmen are perpetual optimists. Their optimism holds them in good stead as they fight their way through the trenches and struggle to remain "up." But it can also lull them into a false sense of security, causing a complacent attitude while dealing with customers. It causes the best of us to assume that everything will come out all right. And sometimes it does. We tend to gloss over a problem, to overlook a dangerous warning sign. We ignore the killer objection.

ℂ   TeleSell 7   ℂ

Listen for the Real Objections

Ring . . . Ring . . . Ring.

"Yo?"

"Mr. Granitello, please."

"Speaking."

"Mr. Granitello, Robert Jeffers with the Selmore Corporation. I spoke to you last week about the boxing gloves my company has on sale."

"Who?"

"Jeffers. Robert Jeffers. Remember, I told you about the 'buy twelve and get thirteen' deal on the boxing gloves?"

"Oh, yeah. Sure, I remember you. What can I do for you today?"

"You asked me to get back to you today. I was wondering how many dozen you wanted us to ship to you? The best price point is at twelve dozen."

"Where are they shipping from?"

"Kalamazoo, Michigan, but don't worry, we're picking up the freight on this order."

"Kalamazoo? How long will it take the order to get to me?"

"Oh, I'm sure it won't take long. Now, then, how many dozen shall I ship?"

"I've got a sale running next Wednesday. Will they be here by then?"

"Could be. And I'm sure you remember that we're giving you an extra thirty days billing on this first order. Now how many dozen will you be needing?"

"When will they actually ship?"

"I'll get this order in today. They'll start processing it in the morning. Did you want all those in the same color?"

"Tell you what, Bob. Why don't you give me a call early next week. I really don't need any gloves right now, but next week, after my sale, I'll look over my inventory position again."

—*Click*

What happened? Robert didn't hear what Rocky was saying. Rocky told Robert, "Yeah, I've got a sale coming up, and yeah, I probably don't have enough gloves in stock, but when will I get these if I give you the order?" Robert, on the other hand, kept telling Rocky everything he didn't care about. He talked about volume, pricing, color, and quantity, but every time the subject of delivery came up, Robert skirted around it. Well now, no answer, no sale. No sale, no commission. Pretty simple stuff. Robert ignored the objection instead of meeting it head on.

There are a great many ways he could have handled the objection successfully. He should have offered to expedite shipping. He should have said he'd walk the order through processing and get it rolling today. He could have suggested express freight and even shown how the extra charges could be absorbed by the terrific deal Rocky was making on the cost of the gloves. There were many options, but instead he chose to ignore the issue, which in turn, caused him to lose the sale. Worse still, Rocky will remember this and never do business with the Selmore Corporation.

Robert Jeffers blew this one.

THE IMPORTANCE OF TROUBLESHOOTING

Objections cannot be ignored. They are as real as a junk-yard dog and twice as deadly. The only way to handle an objection is dead center. Pick it up, turn it over a few times, agree with the customer that the issue certainly is a concern, then resolve the problem to his satisfaction.

While not every problem has a solution, telemarketers are foremost and above all else troubleshooters. We must clear the way for the sale as surely as the pilgrims cleared the forest to build homes. You cannot build a house around a tree, and you cannot build a sale around an objection! Learn this now and save hours of frustration.

©   TeleSell 8   ©

Clearing Objections

Ring . . . Ring . . . Ring.

"Hello."

"Ms. Kettleworth, please."

"Speaking."

"Ms. Kettleworth, Janet Jones here with the Selmore Corporation. Our company is running a promotion on panty hose this month, and we'd like to extend an invitation to you to become a customer of ours. As an introductory package, we'll ship you a free display with each 100 panty hose you purchase and, with each display, we'll also send you a window banner. We handle only name brands and have a full selection of each brand we carry. These point of purchase promos will guarantee that your customer is cognizant of your sale the moment she walks into your store. What do you think?"

"Well, Ms. Jones, it sounds like a fine promotion, but in the summer months we tend to stay away from panty hose sales and stick more to seasonal items."

"I know. So does everyone. Which means that by bucking the trend, you will probably snare more customers and will certainly have the first shot at increasing sales through this forgotten item at summer time."

"True. But space is such a problem this time of year. We have fans, lawn chairs, and ice chests piled all the way to the ceiling. I really don't think we have room for any more floor displays. Why don't you try me again in the fall?"

"In the fall everyone will have displays out! As far as room is concerned, we only need two square feet. The profit those few inches yield will stagger you. After all, women wear panty hose all year long. I'll bet you've got a pair on right now!"

"Good point. Let me think. Maybe I could put displays near the checkout counters. Or . . ."

Get the idea? Janet zeroed in on the main objection her customer had about selling panty hose in the summer. She did not try to gloss it over with statements about the price or packaging. She went right to the heart of the objection. She pointed out that, while space was indeed at a premium, perhaps Kettleworth did not realize how little space was involved. The part about the practicality of selling panty hose all year long was especially well taken when she pointed out that the buyer was probably wearing a pair, even as they spoke. Janet did a good job of clearing the trees before trying to build the house.

Not all objections can be overcome. If a customer says to you that money is tight right now, you can respond by telling him the only way cash loosens up in a retail operation is with the generation of new sales. This can best be accomplished by running a sale on selected merchandise, merchandise which you just happen to sell. If he tells you, however, that his company is about to go into Chapter 11, no amount of salesmanship is going to make this deal fly, nor do you particularly want it to.

When customers tell you they are overstocked with the item you're selling, suggest an in-store promotion to lower their inventory levels. Suggest ways to move the product they already have and ways they can serve their best interests by including merchandise you have for sale. Remember this: *your customer is not in business to help you make your quota,* but if you can help him make his, he can help you make yours!

Assuming you intend to be in the same job for more than thirty-two hours, you will do well to remember that buyers are more like lambs than cattle. You can make a sweater from the same lamb every season, while you can only make a pair of boots from a cow once! As telemarketers, we must set aside our sense of grab-all-we-can, in favor of a more patient, long-term approach. In the final analysis, this is what makes some of us salesmen— true telesellers—and others merely clerks.

The most successful business operations are those that do not take advantage of their customers. Walk into any McDonalds and complain about the Big Mac you bought last night, and you will instantly be given a certificate worth the purchase price of last night's fiasco. Sears will replace any tool it sells, no questions asked, for as long as you own the tool. You don't need a receipt, you don't need a warranty card. Why do these companies do this? The answer is simple. It costs these merchandising giants millions of dollars each year to advertise how important the customer is to them. Does it make sense to alienate one individual who will spend the next week of his life speaking badly of the company? Of course not!

The fact is, it is easier to keep a customer than to make a new one. Long-term relationships make steady business. History! A history with you and with your company. I have relied on this many times when involved in a dispute with an old customer. I have pointed out that in the last ten years that we, he and I together, have never had a problem we could not resolve, evidenced by the fact we were still doing business together.

The important thing to remember is that it is infinitely cheaper to maintain an existing account than to try and find one with which to replace it.

FERRETING OUT THE REAL OBJECTIONS

Not all objections are easy to spot. Often, the customer will not give us the real objection and, at times like this, we have to do a bit of deductive reasoning.

ℂ   TeleSell 9   ℂ

Discerning Price as an Objection (Part 1)

Ring . . . Ring . . . Ring.
"Yo."

"Rocky?"

"Speaking."

"Your friend, Robert, with Selmore."

"Yo, Robert. What's up?"

"Just got a special price on mouth guards. I thought that you might need some."

"Are they ABS or Poly?"

"ABS."

"Boxed?"

"Yep. Four-color printing, with a hangtag to display on a peg rack, or, they'll stack on a counter."

"How many do I have to take?"

"There's only one gross in a deal. How many deals are you interested in?"

"Any special price if I took five deals?"

"I could make you five deals for $288.00 per gross. That works out to $2.00 per unit."

"Just a second, let me check my stock."

(By the way, when a customer puts you on hold, don't engage someone else in your office with idle chitchat. It tends to make you lose your train of thought, leaves open the possibility you will say something you wouldn't want overheard, and also takes away from the intimacy of the call if the customer comes back on the line while you are in midsentence.)

"Yo, Robert. I'm gonna pass. I think I've got plenty of mouth guards in stock. Check with me next month."

—Click

Why did Rocky decline? Robert got shot down by a pricing decision. Even though Rocky said he was passing the deal because of an inventory situation, it was obvious that until the price quote, Rocky was interested. He asked about the composition of the item, the packaging, the quantity in a case, and if there was a special price for larger quantities. There was every indication that the deal was as good as written, when suddenly, after ascertaining the price of the item, Rocky cooled off. Remember, it was Rocky who asked all the questions. He was obviously interested up to the point he figured that the cost was too high.

This situation is very common in phone sales. The fact that the buyer cannot see you works for him too. What Robert could not see was that Rocky picked up a price sheet from Robert's competitor and found the same item 10 percent cheaper.

GETTING A SECOND CHANCE TO MAKE THE SALE

Robert was beaten by the "invisible" objection. There are ways to rebut this type of objection. Learn to recognize this ploy for what it is. Robert was shot down without ever seeing the bullet. To repair the damage this did to his credibility, he must recover quickly and move fast. Let's go back to the end of the conversation:

© _TeleSell 10_ ©

Discerning Price as an Objection (Part 2)

"Yo, Robert. I'm gonna pass. I think I've got plenty of mouth guards in stock. Check with me next month."

"What are you paying for them now?"

"I can get them from the PriceRite Corporation for $259 per gross and only have to take two gross to get that price."

(So there it is. Price! Chances are, Rocky will call his salesman at PriceRite and the other guy will get the benefit of Robert's labor. Robert worked the field, yet another salesman will reap the harvest unless Robert works quickly and recognizes what just took place.)

"Hold on a second, can you, Rocky? My supervisor just walked in. Let me see if I can get you a better price."

(Let Rocky hold for about twenty seconds. He won't mind holding, because he knows the chances are good you're about to get him a better price, thereby saving him money and increasing his gross profit margin. Go back on the line and tell him what you've done.)

"Rocky, my boss is willing to meet the $259 price. Now, did you want five gross or more?"

This technique offers more than just the advantage of saving the sale. The long-term effects are staggering. To begin with, Rocky now knows Robert will go to bat for him. He also subconsciously realizes that Robert is more astute than he first gave him credit. Robert saw right through Rocky's ruse about inventory and was able to correct an objection before it became a sale killer. Keep in mind, you won't get paid for the ones that get away!

WHAT TO DO WHEN YOU DON'T KNOW THE ANSWER

While most objections can be resolved on the spot, there will come a time when the customer has an objection you cannot dispel at that exact moment. He'll want to know, for example, how much a case of a particular item weighs or how it's packed. *If you don't know, don't guess!* Someone in the office has the answer. Tell your customer you'll find out and call him right back. Stop selling at that point!

We've already observed that objections are too dangerous to ignore; therefore, you will deal with it in one of two ways. You can guess the answer or lie. Both are equally as bad.

Another reason to break off the sales call is more subtle in nature. By telling your customer that you will get the information for him, you will establish yourself in his eyes as a dedicated, conscientious salesperson, one worthy of consideration. You will not have blatantly tried to hustle him for a sale. You will have demonstrated to your customer that you are concerned with the issues that concern him.

IN PARTING . . .

The best telemarketers in the world cannot hope to make a sale while objections are ignored. If the problem is too tough or if your company policy is rigidly in opposition to the solution of your customer's problem, then move on to the next customer. There *are* those rare cases in which a problem arises that cannot easily be resolved. Remember that the agony of losing a fish from your hook can be soothed with the knowledge that fish travel in schools. There's always the next call!

four

Defining Objectives in Sales Promotions: Putting Together a Telemarketing Promotion

A promotion is put together for a variety of purposes. Lowering inventory levels, attaining higher discounts from manufacturers, raising cash, or attracting new customers are some of the fundamental reasons behind a limited sales promotion.

What makes a telemarketing promotion successful? Many factors come into play when considering the success of any promotion. First and foremost, the promotion must have a specific goal behind it. Its success is then measured against the objective. For instance, not all sales are run for the purpose of raising cash. A sale can be the first foray into a new field or line of business. Often, promotions are used by companies to introduce new services or products.

If the Selmore Corporation wanted to expand its product line from sporting goods, it would undoubtedly encounter some resistance in the marketplace. But, by placing these new items with an existing account, they can eliminate the first major hurdle of new acquisitions, that of, "Who'll buy the new line?"

PLACING NEW PRODUCTS AND LINES

Robert Jeffers already sells the buyer, Rocky, all the gloves and mouth guards Good Sports can use. If Robert wants to capitalize on his already established relationship with Good Sports, he must bring in new products Good Sports will need. Robert can continue to search out and buy new sporting goods, or he can examine other needs his customers might have. What about office equipment and supplies? Good Sports must use an incredible amount of plastic sacks to bag their goods when they make a retail sale, and these sacks are being bought from someone. Why not Robert? But for Robert's company to get a good price on these sacks, thereby remaining competitive in the marketplace, they will need to purchase them in huge quantities.

For the Selmore Corporation to break into the plastic bag business, they must have a viable market for their new product. They will have to look toward their established customers for new product distribution. Marketing these bags to an already established customer, Good Sports, will mean they must give Good Sports a lower price than they now receive from their current vendor. If not a lower price, something else must be offered to the customer to make switching vendors profitable and worthwhile.

The hook could be free freight, it could be volume pricing at less than volume quantities, or it could be something as simple as appealing to a one-stop shopping concept. But there must be some solid reason to sway Good Sports away from their current vendor. They are, after all, going to risk losing their supplier once they begin to buy Robert's new line. To introduce the new product success-fully, Robert will have to run a promotion. If this promo-tion is successful, he will sell a lot of plastic bags. More importantly, he will widen his line, thereby greatly in-creasing his chances of a sale when he calls his good friend, Rocky, for an order.

The rationale here is quite simple. If a man sells only apples, then he has an average chance of making a sale every time one of his customers needs apples. If he sells oranges in addition to apples, then his chances for a sale to any one customer double. Moreover, as a vendor of two types of produce, he becomes more convenient to buy from. When he adds bananas and grapes to his line, his value to his customer increases proportionately. But, all of these items are in the same line and, on a broader scale, he is still selling only produce. If the produce market becomes soft, or worse, depressed, then he has little chance of re-couping his investment. *The bottom line is that the opportu-nity to sell rises in direct proportion to your ability to serve your customer's needs.*

I have found that the more items I can bring to my customer's desk, the more receptive he is toward my lines. The reason is obvious. If a buyer purchases fifty different items from fifty different vendors, then a large part of his day is spent contacting and being contacted by his fifty sources. If, however, he can buy five different items from each supplier, he then need deal with only ten different companies. The buyer saves time; his need to remain fa-miliar with fifty different companies is reduced by 80 per-cent. This makes for a more effective buyer and, ulti-mately, a better customer. Instead of being a small fish to fifty different salesmen, he becomes a large fish to ten. The telemarketer who can satisfy this buyer's needs is more likely to garner a larger share of the business and will be-come, in turn, a stronger source for the buyer.

With the addition of each new item to the line and each new line to the program, you strengthen and reinforce the concept of one-stop shopping. If you think this concept doesn't work, walk into any large grocery chain in America. From aardvark feed to Xerox® supplies, you can spend three hours shopping and seldom leave without almost every shopping need being filled.

Before Selmore Corporation can become a merchandising giant, Robert is going to need to sell Rocky some plastic bags. And before Robert can entice Rocky into buying these bags, Selmore Corporation will need to launch a major telemarketing drive to interest enough people in their new line. Without customer support, volume purchasing will not be possible, and therefore, competitive pricing will be unattainable. It is volume purchasing that makes this type of line profitable. First the bait, then the fish.

USING TELEMARKETING PROMOTIONS TO IDENTIFY PROSPECTIVE NEW CUSTOMERS

One of the main objectives behind a phone promotion is to identify and secure new customers. In this respect, telemarketing is no different than any other method of sales. New customers are the lifeblood of any organization. Even the best of customer bases will erode over time. Death, bankruptcies, change of ownership, bad times, misunderstandings and, of course, competition, all take their toll on any customer base. The only way a company can protect against customer erosion is to constantly add new customers and new orders.

In Miami, a national electronic distributor maintains two separate mailing lists. The first list is the "A" list. It's comprised only of established accounts, people who buy on a regular or semiregular basis. The second list, the "B" list, is made up entirely of prospective customers. It con-

sists of the names, addresses, and phone numbers of people they would like to have as customers. These businesses
have inquired about their lines, but have not as yet bought
from the firm.

The Miami distributor maintains two different promotions at all times. Twice a month they mail sale fliers to
both lists. The "B" list, however, receives flyers which have
substantially lower prices. They do this for two reasons.
First, and most obviously, unusually lower prices can more
easily make a convert out of someone else's customer. Lure
them in with lower prices, and once they are regular
customers, gradually go back to the regular price. Second,
even if the promotion does not result in recruiting a new
customer, the lower prices listed on the sale flier will certainly make the competition look bad.

PLACING YOUR CUSTOMER OUT OF THE REACH
OF YOUR COMPETITION

Another reason to run a promotion, especially a seasonal
one, is to load up customers with merchandise, even at a
reduced profit, and take the customer out of the market.
This puts them out of reach of the competition—at least
for the time being. With luck, you have also spoiled the
chances for the competition to sell any related items to the
customer as well. The odds are, if Selmore is able to take
Good Sports out of the market for tennis shoes, then a
competitor would have little encouragement to pursue
Good Sports if all they are buying is shoelaces. Good
Sports becomes an unattractive customer based solely on
the fact they will not be buying for the next three months
or more. By blocking a competitor from getting his foot in
the door, Selmore has hurt the competition while increasing sales for itself.

USING DIRECT MAIL IN TELEMARKETING PROMOTIONS

Every successful telemarketing promotion should begin with the written word. A well-placed sale circular has the impact of a television commercial with the relative expense of a classified ad. Any promotion conducted by a telemarketing firm should begin with a sale flier. This flier need not be confined to the conventional medium generally used to advertise limited or seasonal specials. The conventional medium would call for the mailing of a four-page advertisement with specials printed in large type. Maybe included in the copy would be information such as packaging, size, and weight.

But this is a self-limiting approach to the marketplace, and it's expensive. Let's consider the Selmore Corporation's "annual preinventory, once-in-a-lifetime, super sale," during the last week in December. It is no surprise to the customers who regularly avail themselves of the bargains offered by the Selmore Corporation that this sale is being repeated for the tenth consecutive year. And it's no surprise that the items they paid full price for two weeks earlier are reduced up to 25 percent. The way in which Selmore is announcing this sale is a surprise however.

The Postcard

Instead of the usual four-page sales catalog, dealers on Selmore's customer list will this year get only a postcard. The card will have a message printed on the back and be hand addressed, posted with a stamp, not a meter.

The reason for hand postage, rather than a machine, is that anything which makes your mail stand out from all the other cards, letters, and advertisements that your customer receives every day gives you an advantage. For this reason I find that using stamps, especially commemorative postage with pictures depicting any unusual scene, such as a space launch, a revolutionary war hero, or even a dinosaur, will make my mail distinctive. It takes a bit more time to prepare this type of mailing, but if it causes your customer to remember it, then it's well worth the effort.

The same thing goes for hand-addressing the card. There are few things more personal in the business world than a hand-addressed letter. Whenever I sort my mail, I tend to put anything handwritten toward the top of the stack.

Robert's postcards will look like the following. On the front, in handwriting, will be:

Robert Jeffers
Selmore Corp.
P. O. Box 4257
N. Y., N. Y., 10006

Mr. Rocky Granitello
Good Sports Store
1412 Kings Place
Denver, Co., 88665

Attention: Rocky

On the back, printed by computer or word processor:

Rocky,

I will be calling you during the week of December 26-31. I have a list of the lowest prices of the year. Don't buy anything until you hear from me. You'll be glad you waited.

Kindest regards,

Robert Jeffers
Selmore Corporation

Many things will cross Rocky's desk that week, but I guarantee you, Robert's postcard will remain on top of his incoming basket until he receives the call he was told was coming. The effect of this simple card is unbelievable.

When Robert calls Rocky, he will find a customer waiting to be sold. Compare this to the four-page specials list he received from the competition at PriceRite and the advantage becomes clear. Excitement builds because the details of the super sale are not yet unveiled. If this is not an exceptional sale, why were the cards hand-addressed and stamped? In an age where machines talk to machines and fax copiers answer your telephone, there is absolutely nothing like a hand-addressed envelope!

When the big day arrives and the phone rings uniting Rocky with his friend Robert, only good things can follow.

USING A MAIL-A-GRAM FOR MAXIMUM EFFECT

A number of years ago Western Union began a campaign to introduce the mail-a-gram as a tool for business. Their claim to fame was the slogan, "The impact of a telegram, for the fraction of the cost." This campaign put Western Union back on the map of successful businesses in the 1970s. It was successful because it was an idea whose time had come. It was successful because businessmen found it innovative, quick, and extremely profitable. In the early 1980s, a company that dealt largely with Radio Shack dealers across the United States made regular monthly use of this medium to announce the advent of a sale or a stock clearance with a success rate that bordered on phenomenal.

The Electronics Distributor would release 400 mail-a-grams over a five-day period, announcing a sale lasting three days from the date of the letter. Each mail-a-gram was followed within forty-eight hours by a phone call. Ninety-three percent of those calls resulted in a sale exceeding the $200 minimum required by company policy. Each call would begin basically the same way:

☎   *TeleSell 11*   ☎

Using the Mail to Promote the TeleSale

Ring . . . Ring . . . Ring.

"Hello."

"Tim Rogers, please."

"Speaking."

"Tim. Your friend, Todd, here. Did you get my mail-a-gram?"

"Yeah, I got it. What's the deal? I didn't get a sale flier, only the note saying you'd call."

"We figured with prices this good, you'd think they were misprints."

The sales representative would then go through a list of merchandise selected for seasonal advantages or line teasing.

HOW TO PROMOTE SALES USING LINE TEASING AND SEASONAL ADVANTAGES

"Teasing the line" means that one or two items are selected from a specific category. These items by themselves would not amount to a well-rounded order but are priced to induce the buyer to begin his order with them and fill it out with other items at the regular price.

For example, a drugstore might be offered a group of lipsticks, in six colors, at a 40 percent discount. There are a total of thirty-six colors in the package, but only six are on sale. Six colors are enough to whet the appetite of the buyer, but he'd need at least eighteen different colors to entice a customer to look and linger over the lipstick display. This means that while he can buy six colors at a discount, he'll need to buy at least twelve and perhaps as many as thirty different colors at the regular price.

Merchandise sold by the seasonal advantage method are items commonly found in stores at special times of the year. Christmas cards in the winter, Easter decorations in the spring, beach balls in summer are all seasonal advantage items. By putting a certain line of Christmas cards on sale, a distributor leaves room to push regular Christmas cards at full price. The psychology here is that the order is already being written, the buyer is already on the phone, the freight is already being considered, why not throw a few more items into the packing cartons?

It is at this point that the phone salesman is at his most profitable posture to the company and, therefore, to himself. He is the point-of-purchase display of which all retailers are so fond. There's a reason why racks of gum and stacks of tabloids are found next to the cash register at grocery stores. They are impulse items the store management hopes will be picked up on the way through the checkout stand.

The phone salesman armed with a sales flier is in the same position. If he sold only the sale items, there would be no need to employ him. The sales flier already advertised the special items. It is his duty to point out other merchandise—other impulse items—to the buyer as he goes through the sale sheets.

IN PARTING . . .

Remember: the very best customer we have is the one on the phone right this minute. The expense of calling him has already been made whether he buys or not. For a few extra minutes, you can ring up more items and increase the size of the ticket in direct proportion to your sales ability. Avoid being too anxious and rushing the buyer; walk him through the warehouse of your mind, telling him about all the goods you think he could use.

A customer who is buying, is one who can buy more!

five

Organization in Telemarketing

The one key ingredient found in all great salesmen, regardless of what they sell or how they sell it: organization is an irreplaceable trait.

I cannot stress enough how absolutely important it is to develop a selling plan. Product knowledge, networking, price strategy, even advertising mean nothing without a salesplan. There are three basic plans which must be mapped out in any successful sales effort. They are: the promotion itself; the sales approach; and the sales effort. Together, these three elements amount to a successful campaign. With the omission of any one factor, almost any endeavor is doomed to failure.

The sale fliers have been in the mail for two days. The warehouse is stocked to the rafters. The credit office is prepared for the deluge of old and new customers placing orders. The phone crew is ready, and Robert is preparing to kick off the "annual preinventory, once-in-a-lifetime, super sale."

Before this super sale gets underway, there are a few things of which we need to be sure. Let's back up to when Robert first sat at his desk this morning. The first step in a successful sales effort is to organize the day.

There are three types of organization: (1) the "seat of the pants" theory; (2) the old-fashioned approach, using customer information cards (CIF); and (3) the computer filing approach.

SELLING BY THE SEAT OF THE PANTS

The random selection of customers, chosen more by experience than by any preordained selection process, is based on years of familiarity between the customer and the salesman. You will not find this mode used by young people or people new to an industry. The salesman who has called the same customers for the last decade and knows their phone numbers from memory is most likely to use this type of selling. It has both advantages and disadvantages.

The primary advantage is familiarity. The "seat of the pants" salesman knows who will buy what. He knows who is in the office and when. He knows who is likely to give big orders. His heavy-hitter list is programmed into his automatic dialer, and he needs about three minutes preparation to begin his day. He'll walk into the office, sit at his desk, and before noon, have sold his quota for the day.

But, as with any great plan, there is a down side. He will prospect very few new customers, and the accounts he has may already be stocked to the gills with merchandise because he has a tendency to call only the sure hits, thereby keeping them well supplied and ignoring the smaller customers. There is in this approach an inherent danger of stagnation, stagnation which will result in burnout more quickly than with any other approach to sales. The net result is spasmodic selling, one week going great guns, the next week scraping the bottom of the barrel to justify a draw.

CUSTOMER INFORMATION FILES

Customer information files (CIF) tend to be bulky and are difficult to manage but often provide the best approach to consistent sales. They are usually arranged in alphabetical order, either by account name or city and filed in a desktop filing box. Long ago I developed a CIF card which I have used ever since. (For a sample of a Customer Information File card, see Exhibit 1, on the following page.)

In the absence of a computerized filing system, the CIF card is as essential to the phone salesman as is "the little black book" to the legendary traveling salesman. Examine it closely.

The information on this card is arranged in order of importance. The first item called for is the day or date of calling. As this chapter unfolds, you will see the need for consistency in calling the prospect. Having the call day on the top of the card is of enormous help when organizing your day. Next comes the time zone information. With phone sales, especially on a national scale, knowing what time it is *where you are calling,* will be of tantamount importance. Your initials on the top, right-hand corner will establish this account as yours and help resolve any confusion which may later occur as a result of an overeager associate's desire to plunder your territory.

The account number, name of the store, buyer's name, phone number, and address need no explanation except that they should be complete and accurate. The line for "prospected" will indicate the first time the buyer was contacted. The next line, marked "freq," indicates how often a customer is to be contacted. This can range from daily, in the case of a heavy hitter, to quarterly, in the case of a large but systematic buyer.

The line for "type of store" identifies the kind of operation the customer maintains. This line will show whether the account is a retail, discount, franchise, or wholesale operation. This information, like all the other data, will save you time and money. It will allow you to target spe-

Exhibit 1

Customer Information File (CIF)

Call Day _____ (Date) _____ Time Zone _____ Salesman _____
Account # _____ Name of Store _____
Buyer _____ Phone (___) _____ Prospected _____
Address _____ City _____ St. _____ Zip ___
Freq. _____ Type of Store _____ Hours _____
Terms _____ Freight _____ Days Off _____
Special Instructions _____
_____
_____

Comments _____
_____
_____

REVERSE SIDE

Date	Items	Qty.	Price	Date	Items	Qty.	Price

cific types of deals for specific markets. If, for example, you designate a particular store to be a "retail-mall" operation, rule out selling them any type of deal which involves bulk or unpackaged merchandise. This type of an operation will be more concerned with packaging—how the product can be displayed and how it can be protected from shop-lifting. While price will be a consideration here, the more important issue for this type of operation is appearance. Such an outfit will be more inclined toward point-of-purchase displays and banner advertisements.

The "hours" line is intended to note when the buyer is in the office, not necessarily when the store is open. "Terms" and "freight" prove valuable when selling a promotion which features extended terms or prepaid freight. The "days off" line will also save you time and money, when blitzing a hot deal.

"Special instructions" and "comments" are of particular use to the phone salesman. Remember, this is not a rigid or structured form. Use this section to record any information which could be useful to you as you grow to know your customer better. In the course of conversation you will discover personal items such as the buyer's birthday or his children's hobbies. Perhaps you will learn such personal things as his wedding anniversary, his wife's name, or the college he attended. Any of these items will be of use to you as you continue your business relationship in the months and years to come. It is unbelievable what one well-placed birthday card can do for your relationship with a buyer. Remember, the telephone is an impersonal instrument. Anything you can do to make it less so will serve you well once you have established a prospect as a client.

You will remember that in the first chapter I discussed the overuse of manners in our industry. I cautioned you not to ask about the health of your prospect or not to begin the conversation by inquiring, "How are you today?" Nothing has changed! The reason you will now seek to personalize your approach is that once you are at the point of using the CIF card you are past the prospect stage and rapidly approaching the confirmed customer stage. You are no longer a stranger to the client, and at some point in the relationship, you will begin to develop a familiarity with him or her. This familiarity is not only permissible, it is desirable. Remember, people do business with their friends before total strangers. In the beginning, in the first fifteen seconds of the first phone call, you were a stranger. By the third call you should have begun to build a relationship, part of which will entail knowing more about him than just his name and position with the company.

The reverse side of the card is double columned, leaving room to enter the date of the last sale, the item(s) purchased, the quantity purchased, and the price paid. This allows Robert to see, at a glance, the last time Rocky bought mouth guards, how many he bought, and what price he paid. It will serve as a reminder to ask Rocky about items he has not purchased recently and also to cue Robert when to mention a sale and, perhaps as important, when not to. If Rocky bought a gross of boxing gloves last week at regular price, it's probably not wise to mention that they are on sale at half price today.

Computer Filing

The only organizational method better than CIF cards is a computer system. But remember, while a computer is a great telemarketing asset, it's not a miracle cure. It can tell you who to call and when; it will even tell you the last time you called, what you sold, and for how much. It cannot make your calls for you. Nothing takes the place of experience. (See Exhibit 2 on the following page for a sample computer customer information file.)

The primary advantage to using a computer in place of manual CIF cards is speed and accuracy. I insert a call day for each of my customers, and when I begin work each morning, all I need do is punch in the day of the week

Exhibit 2

Computer Customer Information File

ACCT:_____ ZONE:_____ OWNER: _____ PHONE: (___) _____

CUSTOMER: _____ TYPE: _____ SALESMAN: _____

ADDRESS: _____ BUYER: _____

CITY: _____STATE: _____ ZIP: _____ TERMS: _____

CALL DAY: _____ FREIGHT: _____

LAST CALL: _____ SPECIAL: _____

COMMENTS: _____

_____

_____

_____

and my computer automatically draws my customer list for the day. If a customer has requested a callback on a day other than his regular day, by noting that in my computer file, I will automatically be informed when I draw my list that day. There is no contest here. The machine has a much better memory than I do—a fact I rely on to draw a complete list each morning.

Of course, there are drawbacks to putting all your notes in one basket. Computer failure, power outages, even sabotage can render you lost, without the necessary tools to do your job. These problems can be mitigated, however, with the use of a backup printout which will provide you with a safety net in the event of computer failure.

Thus armed with his CIF, Robert is ready to plan his day. He should place his cards or draw his list in two phases: 1) in order of availability throughout the day; and 2) in the importance of each client in relation to each other. This would mean that, in the case of a national sales program, the sorting of customers by time zone. He would then arrange these customer cards in the order of importance.

SELLING BY TIME ZONE

Robert's company is located in Denver. By the time he is ready to begin his sales effort at ten o'clock in the morning, it is already noon on the East coast. He would be well advised, therefore, to begin his day with customers located in the Central Time Zone, where it is then only eleven o'clock.

He will work the Central Zone until noon Central Time, shifting then to Mountain Time when he will call local customers between eleven and noon. In the following hour he will shift to the Eastern Time Zone, complete that sector and move on to Central, then local, then Pacific Time Zone, thus completing his day at five o'clock Mountain time, four o'clock Pacific Time.

This is not as confusing as it appears. Common sense is the best guide here. It doesn't take a great deal of reflection to realize most buyers are out of their office during lunch. As Robert becomes more familiar with his clientele, he will learn the best times to call each customer. He learned that Rocky seldom took calls first thing in the morning and was in a better frame of mind later in the day. With a simple notation on his CIF, Robert understood that to sell Rocky he needed to call a half hour after the man came back from lunch. He fine-tuned his calls to his customer's needs.

After arranging the cards in order of time zones, the next phase of the organization process is to place the sorted cards in some order as to yield the greatest amount of sales as early in the day as possible. It is important that your day start out well. If you place the better customers in the early slots and the tougher ones in the later ones, you will develop a pattern of successful calls early in the day. This can give you the impetus needed to keep you going when the clients become less responsive later in the day. There is a tendency, however, to put all your good customers first and leave the "toughies" till the end of the day. I would advise against this. Telemarketing is a difficult job. I have heard it likened to a day in the desert. Like any trek across a desert, one is well advised to leave little canteens of water, i.e. good customers, scattered at various points along the trail.

IN PARTING . . .

Remember: Robert must impart to Rocky the same sense of urgency he himself feels for his product. He must motivate Rocky to the point that Rocky sees the sale as a mutually beneficial experience. Nobody, not a single soul, will buy from Robert just because Robert is having a bad day. There are times when Robert will be able to appeal to his customer's sense of fair play, to his inherent desire to be friendly and helpful, but as a rule, playing the role of the underdog will get Robert what dogs usually get. Leftovers!

It is for this reason that Robert will need to get himself motivated before he makes his first call. Make sure the first call is not to a hostile voice. *Do not, under any circumstances, allow your first call of the day to be to someone you know in your heart will not buy from you today.* Try to get started on an up note and your day will follow through along the same track. This is not to say that if your first customer turns you down, seek a rafter upon which to hang yourself. Just get a strong start as soon as possible. Leave the dead wood until later in the day where it can do the least amount of damage.

six

Setting Yourself Up for a Successful Day

There is no doubt that the customer can sense your mental attitude on the phone. If you are on a roll and sales are breaking for you as they should, your voice will exude a tone of confidence. If they are not, if you are finding new meaning for the phrase "pulling teeth," they can sense that too. I've had customers say to me, "Aren't you feeling well today?" There was nothing wrong with me physically. What they heard in my voice was fatigue, panic, and mental strain as I realized I was not going to make my quota.

There is a school of thought that believes the better a salesman dresses, the fancier his auto, the more jewelry on his hand, the more a customer has confidence in him. After all, he wouldn't be successful if his product wasn't good. Therefore, he is successful because his customers are a success, and they are a success because his product was a success. See the story here? Success breeds success.

A phone salesman cannot impress his customer with a diamond watch, and if he were to mention it, the customer wouldn't believe he has one anyway. Rocky can't see Robert's German sports car or his country club membership. What Rocky can and will sense is Robert's attitude. If Robert is up, he has a much better chance of involving Rocky in the program. If he is down, Rocky will respond accordingly.

THE DAILY BATTLE FOR SALES

One fact outshines all others in the business of selling. Yesterday's sales are old news! There is perhaps no other field of endeavor where the pressure is as great to prove yourself all over again every day. Doctors are assumed to be brilliant surgeons if they perfect one new technique. Lawyers can ride on the coattails of a single successful case for years. Politicians need win an election only once every few years. But a salesman's reputation and esteem is on the line every time he sits at his desk and picks up the phone. No one cares what you did yesterday. Not your boss, not your mate. Yesterday, you got lucky. Now, to prove it wasn't a fluke, you have got to do it again!

It isn't fair, but it's just the way it is. So the task at hand is to be able to do it, not only one *more* time, but *every* time we practice our art. (And, it never gets any easier.) I'm not telling you anything you didn't already know, I'm just telling you something you probably haven't thought about in a long while. You are a professional salesman, and you're ready for today's challenge. How are you going to do it today?

DEVELOPING THE RIGHT ATTITUDES

The first thing you are going to do is develop a positive attitude about the task that lies ahead. Why are you here while other men labor in hot factories and dig coal out of dark mines? You are here because, like any other successful person, you are a master at your craft. Like any other master, you constantly strive to perfect your craft.

As we discussed earlier in this book, preparation is the key to success. To that end, you must have a daily regimen that, while allowing for the fact nothing ever goes completely according to plan, will allow you to achieve the goals you set when you arrived at the office this morning.

THREE SEGMENTS OF THE SALES DAY

I have found it easiest to divide every day into three sections: yesterday's business; today's business; and tomorrow's business. Everything I do will fall into one of these three general categories. The overwhelming portion of the day, at least seventy percent, is spent on today's business. Twenty percent is spent on tomorrow's business, while about ten percent is allocated for completing yesterday's affairs.

Today's business is making sales, writing orders, and servicing customers. Yesterday's business is returning calls which came in too late to handle, confirming orders from customers who requested such, and recalling customers who asked to be called today although their calling time is at an earlier period.

Tomorrow's business is prospecting new accounts and planning sales promotions and drives. It also includes calling those customers who requested callbacks tomorrow. Consider tomorrow the day that never gets here. Rest assured, no matter what you accomplish today, something will be left over to start tomorrow anew.

Try to see each day as a meal. Some of what you ate was left over from yesterday's dinner. Most of what you are served will be fresh today, and what you do not finish today will be served again tomorrow.

CHECK THE LIST

Here is a list of items Robert will need to do his job today. Before the receiver is lifted from the phone, make sure all these things are present on your desk:

- ❑ Several pens or pencils
- ❑ An order pad
- ❑ A time zone chart
- ❑ Area code chart
- ❑ Your company catalog
- ❑ Sale sheet or specials
- ❑ CIF cards, sorted in order of use
- ❑ A clock
- ❑ A stopwatch
- ❑ A clean writing area
- ❑ A sales fix sheet

PREPARING TO SELL

When Robert arrived at his desk this morning, his first order of business, after any sales meetings, was to draw his daily customer list. If he's using CIF cards, he sorted them, searching out the ones marked "Monday." He arranged these in order of time zones and, finally, in order of calling within each zone. He next prepared his list of specials—the items he wants to promote. He cleared his desk of anything not pertaining to the business at hand. He was ready to do battle.

As his day wears on, Robert will chart his progress on a fix sheet. He will divide the customers on his list into morning and afternoon buyers. However, to be truly effective, a portion of his day will be devoted to customer maintenance. Robert must devote at least one hour to the prospecting of new accounts and the revitalization of old ones.

I prefer to do this right after lunch. Unless I have a particularly busy afternoon planned, I begin prospecting around one o'clock and continue until I have either found a new customer or until I have spent an hour trying. No contact is wasted. Every person spoken to is a potential buyer. If interested, I send them literature. If not, I ask them who in their town might be. Later I will go into greater detail explaining how to use prospecting techniques.

THE IMPORTANCE OF CALLBACKS

Robert is sitting at his desk. He consults his notes from yesterday and schedules in callbacks he must make. Callbacks fall into three general categories: first, the absent buyer; next comes the busy buyer; and last, the dodging buyer. If a customer usually called on Mondays is absent when you call at the regular time, determine when he will be back at his desk. If he is on vacation or sick most secretaries will advise you accordingly.

For the most part, however, you will find he is expected back eventually. If that information is shared with you, you reschedule the call until then. A word of advice here. It is totally useless to call a buyer on his first day back from an extended absence. I wish I had a nickel for each buyer who has told me, "I've been gone a week and don't have the first clue as to what I need."

The way around this objection, however, is quite simple. Knowing the objection beforehand, beat the buyer to the punch. Try:

✆   *TeleSell 12*   ✆

The Touch Base Phone Call

Ring . . . Ring . . . Ring.

"Prescott, here."

"Mr. Prescott. Robert Jeffers with Selmore Corporation."

"Oh, hello Robert."

"Say, I heard you were on vacation. Glad to be back?"

"I'll tell you, Robert. The place is a madhouse. I've got a week's worth of mail to sort out and fifty memos to answer."

"I thought it might be like that today. I only called to remind you I'd be calling you in the morning, unless there's something you need today?"

"No, nothing comes to mind. But do call me in the morning. I'll see what I need by then."

—Click

Wasted phone call? No, indeed! Robert gave Prescott two things he sorely needs. Time and respect. There was a great deal of truth to what he told Robert. He didn't know what he needed today. But, by tomorrow when Robert calls him back, he'll have a much better idea of his needs. And he will remember that Robert did not pressure him on a day when every other person in the world did.

The next category of callback is the busy buyer. This individual is truly too busy to talk right now. Do not take offense to being put off. As I said in the first chapter, the phone is not a respecter of any activity. It may well be true that your buyer is too busy at the moment to take your call. Cooperate with him. When he asks if you can call him back, you really have only two choices. You can say "no," which defeats the purpose of the call to begin with. Or you can say, "Absolutely! What time is good for you?"

There is a strong advantage to calling back at the time he asks. By having you call back, your buyer has more or less obligated himself to hearing you out on the next call. More times than not, this will result in a sale on the return call.

The third type of callback is the dodging buyer. He has no intention of talking to you now or later, if he can help it. There's no cure for him, except to eventually cross him off your list. In time, he will either come around to your calls, or you will drop him. Only time will tell.

Try to schedule callbacks late into the afternoon. They won't interfere with your continued progress and could end up giving your sales effort a boost at the end of a tough day.

DEVELOPING QUOTAS AND BUDGETS

Before the day is done Robert must attain a goal or quota. If Robert's sales manager does not set one, then he must set one for himself. *Quotas are important!* Salespeople need quotas to measure their forward progress. This is as true for the individual salesman who works out of his home as it is for the person who works on the eightieth floor of a building in Manhattan. A quota should be realistic, but challenging. Think of it as a racetrack. There should be enough track to allow a good workout, but not so much as to overwhelm the runner.

The best quotas have basis in fact. Robert draws his by using a number of variables. He set his April quota at $80,000. This is based on the fact last April Robert sold $69,500. His goal this year is to sell 15 percent more than last year, thereby keeping his commissions well ahead of inflation. There are factors, Robert has learned, that influence his daily sales. Time of month, weather, customer composition, seasonal variables, conventions, and number of selling days in a month. All of these tend to change or shift as the year progresses. These changes are taken into account when composing a sales quota or budget.

In Robert's industry, because of Christmas sales and fall sporting activities, at least 40 percent of his business will come in the last quarter of the year. His other high-volume season is the last month of spring and the first month of summer. He will do at least another 25 percent of his quota in these two months. This means five months of the selling year are responsible for almost 65 percent of his sales. The other seven months will net him the other 35 percent.

Last year Robert sold $1.4 million in goods. His goal this year is $1.61 million, allowing for the 15 percent increase he is seeking. April is one of the seven slow months which comprise 35 percent of his yearly sales. He will therefore figure 35 percent of $1.61 million ($563,500) and divide by one-seventh to arrive at his monthly quota for April. His April sales quota stands at $80,000.

Next, because the vast majority of Robert's customers are small corner store businesses, he knows that in the first ten days of the month these clients incur most of their budget expenses, such as rent, sales tax, utility bills, and so forth. Experience has taught him that he will do only about 45 percent of his monthly sales during the first half of the month, with the second half yielding him the other 55 percent. This year April has only twenty-two selling days. By dividing the total quota of $80,000 into two sections, 45 percent for the first half and 55 percent for the second half, his month looks like this:

First Half	$36,000
Per day (11 days)	$ 3,273
Second Half	$44,000
Per day (11 days)	$ 4,000
Total for April	$80,000

Since the month began on a Wednesday, the first week was only three days long. Some sales organizations end their month at the calendar close. Others find it better to close on the same day of the month, such as on the last Friday. This method has the disadvantage of causing the month to start on a Monday, regardless of the calendar date. The end result is a gerrymandering of statistics. In the final study, it does not result in a more even month, only a more predictable last day. Robert's company uses the last calendar day to end their month, hence the first selling day of the new month is always on the first business day of that month.

Many sales organizations have a tendency to "borrow" a few days from one month or "lose" a few days from the current month in order to make their sales seem more consistent. I have serious problems with this. It is important that the telemarketer have a clear concept of how much time he has in a month, how many days he has in a selling period. It does precious little good for a salesperson to work out a sales budget if, in the final analysis, the sales manager will rearrange the month to suit some artificial constraint placed on his department because of accounting needs.

Robert has calculated the number of days in the month, adjusted for a slight upswing in sales toward the second half of each monthly period and has now drawn a budget for April.

The budget outlined in Exhibit 3 is not just an exercise in number crunching. If Robert has any hope of achieving his quota, he needs to watch these figures like a banker watches interest rates. To this end, anything that keeps Robert conscious of his sales budget is time well spent. It is for this reason that Robert will chart his sales not only by the week and day, but by the hour as well.

CHARTING PROGRESS WITH A FIX SHEET

Robert will set up his daily fix sheet and, by watching it closely throughout the day, will constantly find himself

---

Exhibit 3

Monthly Sales Budget for April
Total Projected Sales ($80,000)

Date	Daily	Total	%
April 1	$3,273	$3,273	4%
April 2	$3,273	$6,546	8%
April 3	$3,273	$9,819	12%
April 6	$3,273	$13,092	16%
April 7	$3,273	$16,365	20%
April 8	$3,273	$19,638	24%
April 9	$3,273	$22,911	28%
April 10	$3,273	$26,184	33%
April 13	$3,273	$29,457	37%
April 14	$3,273	$32,730	41%
April 15	$3,273	$36,003	45%
April 16	$3,999	$40,002	50%
April 17	$3,999	$44,001	55%
April 20	$3,999	$48,000	60%
April 21	$3,999	$51,999	65%
April 22	$3,999	$55,998	70%
April 23	$3,999	$59,997	75%
April 24	$3,999	$63,996	80%
April 27	$3,999	$67,995	85%
April 28	$3,999	$71,994	90%
April 29	$3,999	$75,993	95%
April 30	$3,999	$79,992	100%

---

fighting harder to make his daily quota. If he takes care of his days, the week, month, and quarter will take care of themselves.

A fix sheet is only as good as the attention you give to it. Some argue that it's a distraction of a salesman's time, that his main job is to sell, not keep books. They are wrong! A truck driver would never presume to cross the nation without consulting his maps. Nor would an electronic technician tear into a solid-state television without first glancing at the schematics made for the unit. Why, therefore, should a salesman not chart his progress and, from time to time, consult the chart to make sure he is on target?

A fix sheet is nothing more than the daily log of sales, figured on an hourly basis. The fix sheet has more than just one use, however. These sheets can be bound together and, over a period of time, provide a blueprint of the telemarketer's high and low points. They will point Robert toward which part of the day he is more successful and which days of the week he experiences the greatest increase in sales. With proper study, the fix sheet is a very useful tool for Robert (see Exhibit 4, on the following page).

This sheet can be adapted for any industry, and the hours, of course, can be changed to suit the particular needs of any sales force. The simplicity of the sheet makes it very unobtrusive, and the usefulness of seeing an actual diagram of the sales for a day can have an incredible effect toward increasing sales.

IN PARTING . . .

I firmly believe that the key to a successful day of selling begins with the development of an organized approach to the day. Planning, charting, and execution are the three steps each of us must follow to reach the goals we have set for ourselves. The need to lay out a plan at the beginning

Exhibit 4

The Fix Sheet

The Fix			
Date: _____ Day: _____			
Salesman: _____ Quota: _____			

Time	Sales	Aggregate	% of Day
10:00			
11:00			
12:00			
2:00			
3:00			
4:00			
5:00			
6:00			

PERCENT OF QUOTA FOR DAY: _____
AMOUNT OF SALES FOR DAY: _____

of the day is obvious. By charting our progress on an hourly as well as daily basis, we will know where we are throughout the day, the week, and the month. Following our plans and charting our progress will allow us the satisfaction at the end of each day of knowing we are "on track"!

seven

How to Prospect Cold Leads

Up to now we have studied the mechanics of how a phone salesman does his job. There is another, less mechanical aspect to telemarketing, however, which involves intuition and initiative. Coupled with intelligence and common sense, these traits can help form the foundation of a successful telemarketer.

We watched Robert call his customers and winced as he committed mistake after mistake. Let's leave Robert for the time being and introduce Hector—new to the sales game.

This is *day one* for Hector. He starts fresh today with no previous experience, no established accounts, and only a rudimentary knowledge of the product he is going to sell.

The company he works for is the Big Bang Novelty Company. They specialize in the distribution of various novelty items, ranging from salt and pepper shakers to full size bookcases, complete with lights and glass covers. They are in the business of buying and selling merchandise and have developed their own brand, "Bibana." Almost every item they market carries this trademark. They maintain two warehouses, one in California and one in Florida. Their offices are located in New York.

In hopes of avoiding repetitious instructions, I will assume that Hector has been standing over my shoulder reading as I wrote the first section of this book. He has learned from Robert all that Robert knows and is ready to start from this point, armed with the few pearls of wisdom he's already gleaned from the first six chapters.

Today, Hector sits at his desk with a phone, order forms, a few sharp pencils, a calculator, and a yellow legal pad on which to make notes. Also on his desk is a catalog published by the Big Bang Novelty Corporation.

Hector was hired by Ernie Chill, the sales manager for Big Bang. Ernie liked Hector well enough to give him a chance to prove himself. He has confidence in this young man. He's willing to give him as much time as he needs to get established and to begin a buyer-seller relationship with the hundreds of thousands of businessmen across America. He'll give Hector two weeks.

When Ernie hired Hector, he was given a thorough orientation in the products Big Bang has in inventory. This, coupled with promises of "leads," should result in making Hector an overnight success. Typical of the training most phone solicitors receive, all this took the smaller part of one morning. By lunch, Ernie gave Hector a stack of lead cards, most of which came from a trade show Big Bang attended two years ago. On these cards are the names of people who registered for a free vacation in Hawaii. Needless to say, these are not a compilation of the winners of that trip. The cards contain, in the handwriting of the contestant, the contestant's name, company name, address, and office phone number.

Leads this old are not what one would call prime prospects. But they are all Hector is apt to get right now, and this is all he will have to work with. If he can do anything with these, he will get better leads; if not, then Ernie will rely on the old adage, "nothing ventured, nothing gained."

GETTING THE RIGHT PERSON ON THE PHONE

Hector picks up the first card. It reads:

```
                  Mr. Lester Moore
                  Reynolds Company
                  1717 Sycamore Dr.
                  Dallas, TX 77471
                  Phone: (214) 555-7885
```

Hector reaches for the phone. He dials the number on the card.

☎   TeleSell 13   ☎

Knowing Who to Ask For

Ring . . . Ring . . . Ring.

"Renyolds Company, may I direct your call?"

"Mr. Moore, please."

"I'm sorry, Mr. Moore is no longer with us. Can someone else help you?"

"No. Thank you."

—*Click*

What Hector did not realize is, though Lester no longer works for the Reynolds Company, someone else is doing Lester's job. It would have been simple to determine who that person is. Moreover, Lester is probably still working somewhere, and wherever that is, he is probably still a buyer. Hector missed two chances here. The call should have gone like this.

☏   *TeleSell 14*   ☏

Obtaining Information

Ring . . . Ring . . . Ring.

"Reynolds Company, may I direct your call?"

"Mr. Moore, please."

"I'm sorry, but Mr. Moore is no longer with us. May someone else help you?"

"Possibly. Who's taken over Mr. Moore's duties?"

"That would be Mr. Fields. Shall I ring his office for you?"

"Thank you."

Ring . . . Ring . . . Ring.

"Mr. Fields's office."

"Mr. Fields, please."

"May I tell him who's calling?"

"Hector Holt, with Big Bang."

"One moment, please."

See the difference? Hector is still on the same call, but now he's about to speak to Mr. Fields, Mr. Moore's successor. Hector did everything right. He recovered from the faux pas of asking for a person who no longer works for the company (the only person who knows that *he* did not know is the switchboard operator). He got to the buyer's secretary and was straightforward and honest in his dealing with her. She did not feel it necessary to screen this call.

One of the worst things a telemarketer can do is alienate the person who screens the calls. Nothing sounds more suspicious to the screener than someone trying to pass himself off as a friend of the person he is calling. If he had said, "Just tell him Heck is on the phone," he might have gotten through, but the next time he called, he would have gone through Hell trying to talk to Fields.

© *TeleSell 15* ©

Changing Buyers

"Bob Fields, may I help you?"

"Mr. Fields. My name is Hector Holt. I'm with Big Bang Novelty in New York. We had an inquiry from Mr. Moore when he was with your company about some of our products and never got a response to the literature we sent. Do you have our latest catalog?"

"What was the name of your company?"

"Big Bang Novelty."

"No. I don't remember seeing it. What do you sell?"

"Our company markets a large number of novelty and houseware items under the trade name, 'Bibana.'"

"No. Sorry. I'm not familiar with your company. I took this job four months ago, and when I got here things were a mess. Would you mind sending me another one? Mark it to my attention."

"Be glad to. We have several different product lines. What departments do you buy for?"

"Mostly housewares, some giftware."

"Fine. I'll see you get our catalog within the next three days. Let me make sure I have the right address. Are your offices still on Sycamore Drive in Dallas?"

"That's right. 1717 Sycamore."

"And when would be the best time for me to call you to discuss the catalogs?"

"I'm in conferences all day Tuesdays and Thursdays. Any other day, I'm usually at my office in the early mornings and late afternoons."

"How about if I call you a week from today?"

"Perfect."

"Great. I'll call you then. Bye."

—*Click*

LEARN ABOUT YOUR CUSTOMER BY LISTENING TO WHAT HE SAYS AND DOES NOT SAY

What a great call! Hector made initial contact, got the buyer's name, and now knows a bit about the man. He knows Fields's first name is Bob. He knows he is fairly new at his job with this company and that he can be reached on Mondays, Wednesdays, and Fridays. He knows that while his calls are screened, they are not screened to the point of making the man inaccessible. This is a very important point, for if Hector is to sell to this client, he will first need to reach him.

What else does Hector know? He will learn, as he learns the nature of buyers, that this man leans toward an informal approach. He showed this by the way he came to the phone. He did not answer, "Mr. Fields, speaking." Nor did he say, "Robert Fields, may I help you?" He came on the line saying, "Bob Fields, may I help you?" The use of the familiar form of *Robert* gives a clue to the man's attitude toward not only his job, but also toward himself. He was open and honest in his answers and even volunteered information without being asked. Remember the question Hector asked? "Are your offices still on Sycamore Drive?" Fields responded with, "That's right. 1717."

Being able to listen between the lines is important! When we meet a client face to face, many things become evident. Looks, style, even handshakes give us leads to the nature of the prospect. We observe certain aspects of character by the way the client dresses, by how polished his shoes are, even by the cologne he wears. We see, smell, feel, and hear our new acquaintances. Not so with phone sales. All you can do is listen. Hear what the new clients are about. Inflections, use of language, choice of adjectives, tone of voice all tell us what we cannot see. Hector had a conversation with a nice, polite, interested man. He treated Hector as an equal. In all probability and, with the proper handling, Bob Fields can become a good customer for Hector.

And a good thing too, for Hector is about to call his next prospect.

DEALING WITH THE BUYER WHO HAS NO TIME

ℂ   *TeleSell 16*   ℂ

The Customer Who Is Too Busy to Talk

Ring . . . Ring . . . Ring.

"Gilmore and Company, may I help you?"

"Mr. Stringer, please."

"Stringer here."

"Mr. Stringer?"

"Yeah, it's Stringer. What do you want?"

"Mr. Stringer, my name is Hector Holt, and I'm with the Big Bang Novelty Company."

"Call me back later. I'm busy."

—*Click*

Any momentum Hector built from the call to Bob Fields was lost when he talked to Stringer. Stringer was rude, and unfortunately for Hector, there is no way for him to vent the feelings Stringer created. This is a common problem in phone sales. The buyers are sometimes rude, and once they have hung up the phone they go about their business with not another thought of how their inconsiderate attitude will affect the recipients of that rudeness.

Stringer revealed a great deal about himself in these few seconds. He considers himself above common courtesy. Basically he considers himself, and he may very well be, an unusually busy man, a man of little time and great importance. If this is the case, Hector can still talk to him, only his approach will have to be changed. He will have to meet Stringer on Stringer's turf and play the game by Stringer's rules.

The next time Hector calls Stringer, the call should go like this:

© *TeleSell 17* ©

Pushing Past the Brush-Off

"Stringer."

"Mr. Stringer, Hector Holt with Big Bang. We're running a special promotion on salt and pepper shakers, buy six dozen, get one dozen free. Do you have our latest catalog?"

"What's the name of your company?"

"Big Bang. You stopped at our booth at a trade show last year. Filled out an buyer's information card. Do you have our catalog?"

"No. I probably threw it out. Send me a new one. I don't need any shakers right now. Bye."

"Mr. Stringer, what time do you get to work?"

"What?"

"What time do you get to work in the mornings?"

"Six-thirty. Why?"

"I knew you got there early. I can tell you're a busy man. I'll send you the catalogs, and I'll call you earlier in the day next time."

"Yeah, sure. Call me around eight. I usually have more time then."

—*Click*

The difference here is that this time Hector cut right to the chase and told Stringer about a special before Stringer had a chance to shut him out. Hector still did not make a sale but is a lot closer than he was. He knows more about this buyer than before. He knows the man gets to work before Hector gets out of bed. This could account for his lack of manners by two o'clock in the afternoon. At a time many go to lunch, Stringer has already worked seven hours. In a subtle way, Hector paid the man a compliment. He told him he could tell he was a busy man. Bingo! Someone out there realizes just how busy poor Mr. Stringer is. Someone, even if it was a salesman, realizes Stringer is a man with more work than time. Score one for Hector.

FOLLOWING UP ON PROSPECTING CALLS

Hector has completed two calls, neither resulting in a sale. This is not unusual, nor is it negative. Hector is prospecting, and as in any prospecting, be it for gold or for customers, a lot of dirt is moved before the mother lode is found. The most important thing Hector can do now is to keep accurate records of his calls. He should have already filled out two CIF cards and should have addressed two catalogs. Stapled to the front of each catalog—stapled—not paper clipped or taped, should be a note from Hector. In essence, it should say:

Bob,

Here's the catalog you requested. Look through it, and I'll call you next Monday around ten to answer any questions you may have. Hope you have a great weekend.

Regards,

Hector Holt
Big Bang Novelty

This informal note will set the tone for next week's conversation. It serves the dual purposes of reinforcing today's conversation and setting a written appointment for the follow-up call. Today is Monday. Speed is of the utmost importance now. If the mail room dallies with this catalog, and it doesn't leave the office until Wednesday or Thursday, chances are Bob will not have it until Tuesday or Wednesday of next week. This will, although unfairly, cast doubts on Hector's ability to deliver the goods. If he cannot get a catalog out quickly when a possible sale is in the balance, why should Bob expect him to expedite an order?

Never promise a prospect you will mail something and fail to do it. Never say you will call and not call. It will ruin your chances of making a sale, and unlike baseball, you often get only one turn at bat. But, as stated in the beginning of this chapter, Hector is reasonably bright and motivated. He will make sure the catalogs are in the mail at the end of business today.

THE FOLLOW-UP PHONE CALL

Next comes the follow-up. It will probably go like this:

© *TeleSell 18* ©

Following Up on a Mailing

Ring . . . Ring . . . Ring.

"Reynolds Company."

"Bob Fields, please."

"Bob Fields's office."

"Bob Fields, please."

"May I tell him who's calling?"

"Hector Holt, with Big Bang. He's expecting my call."

"Bob Fields, may I help you?"

"Bob, this is Hector with Big Bang Novelty. I sent you a catalog last week, and you asked me to call today. What did you think of the catalog?"

"Ah . . . right. The catalog. I got it around here somewhere. Let me see if I can find it. What's your company again?"

"Big Bang. I sent the book in a large, white envelope with green tabs all around it."

"Right. Here it is. Big Bang Novelty, New York, New York. Got it right here. I'll tell you though, to be honest, I haven't had the chance to study it very closely. Could I get you to call me back later in the week?"

"Absolutely! I was only checking to make sure you received it. I know you'll be in conferences tomorrow, how about if I call you early Wednesday morning?"

"That'll be great. I'll talk to you then. Bye."

—*Click*

How good was that call? Overall, it was a positive step toward making a sale. It reinforced the connection between Hector and Bob. It gave Hector a chance to sound benevolent by not pushing Bob for a commitment, which would have been useless inasmuch as Bob had not yet opened the envelope the catalog came in. More importantly, it revealed to Bob the fact that Hector listened to what he said last Monday about his schedule on Tuesdays and Thursdays. Hector scored big points here—without being obvious.

Bob still sounds like a good prospect and is still worth the time and effort to nurture. Hector will record this second call on his CIF card and refile Bob until Wednesday. Now, it's time to recall our less-than-friendly Mr. Stringer.

ASKING THE RIGHT QUESTIONS

Hector is operating at a disadvantage here because, during the course of the first two calls to Stringer, he failed to get Stringer's first name. Now, when he calls again, he will have to ask for and speak to the formal *Mr. Stringer!* Even worse, he remembers Stringer is a man with little use for politeness or manners:

ℂ   *TeleSell 19*   ℂ

Persisting without Badgering

Ring . . . Ring . . . Ring.

"Gilmore and Company."

"Mr. Stringer, please."

"Stringer."

"Mr. Stringer, Hector Holt with Big Bang Novelties. I sent you our catalog last week and wanted to check to see if there was anything in it you needed."

"Didn't see a thing. Sorry."

"You did get the catalog?"

"Yep, I got it. Just don't need anything right now. Call me back later, though. May need something some other time. Thanks for calling."

"Mr. Stringer, wait. I need to ask you one question."

"I've got people waiting on me, son, what is it?"

"Did I do something wrong? Are you mad at me or my company? I feel like I did something that offended you."

"What? Why would you say that? I'm not mad at anybody! I just don't need anything right now. Call me back later, and I'll see if there's something I can use."

"Sure. When?"

"What?"

"When do you want me to call you back? I'll make a note and call you whenever you think it's a better time."

"Okay, call me next Friday. Early!"

"Yes, sir. Next Friday. You'll be my first call Friday morning. Thank you."

—Click

Hector is getting closer to selling Stringer. He managed what most salesmen never get from Stringer. He made Stringer treat him like a human being, not a disembodied voice. When he calls Stringer back on Friday, Hector will begin the conversation this way:

Ⓒ   TeleSell 20   Ⓒ

Nonconfrontational Demand Mode (Part 1)

"Mr. Stringer, Hector Holt from Big Bang. You asked me to call you this morning so we could go over a few items from my catalog."

Stringer cannot put him off again. After all, it was Stringer who asked Hector to call. Hector must take control and do so in a manner that will not threaten Mr. Stringer's authority. The call will go like this:

Ⓒ   TeleSell 21   Ⓒ

Nonconfrontational Demand Mode (Part 2)

". . . items from my catalog."

"Right, I remember. Well, listen, I didn't see a thing I could use this week. Why not try me again in a few weeks?"

"Mr. Stringer, do you have my catalog handy?"

"It's around here somewhere. Just a second, I'll get it."

"Got it right here."

"If you would, turn to page thirty-one."

"Got it."

"All right. You see the raincoat rack for kids there?"

"I see it."

"Well, Mr. Stringer, I've got a deal for you. For every twelve raincoat racks you take at our regular low price, we'll include a free umbrella stand, worth twelve dollars. This is on top of the fact that all orders over $500 ship prepaid freight. This offer is good regardless of how many racks you buy. It won't be long now before school starts again. These racks are ideal for your back-to-school promotions."

"I suppose that's true."

"How many dozen racks shall I put you down for?"

"No freight on $500?"

"Right!"

"Well, I suppose . . ."

Hector ignored Stringer's attempt to put him off and, instead, moved to a nonconfrontational demand mode. He asked Stringer to produce the catalog, giving him an opportunity to continue the conversation on his terms.

Hector closed the sale! But why? What did he do differently this time than the two calls before? For starters, he lost his fear of rejection. Stringer had already turned him down three times before. In each previous call Hector had been as obliging and deferential as possible. He gave Stringer every opportunity to play nice, but Stringer had no intentions of doing so. In short, Hector had nothing to lose by taking a more aggressive posture. But, make no mistake about this, if Stringer had put his back up, if he told Hector he did not have the time to look up an item in the catalog, this game would have been over.

Stringer is not a bad person or even a rude one. He is typical of many buyers the nation over. He is overworked, underpaid, and doing a job which can cost his company thousands of dollars with every mistake he makes. In his favor, once Hector was able to get past that wall of rejection, once he was able to slow his buyer down long enough to look at the catalog, Stringer turned out to be a fairly decent customer.

For years I had a man like Stringer on my call list. He would start each conversation with me by saying, "I'm busy now, call me later." I must admit it took me longer than three calls to finally realize that later was never going to come. One day I said to him, "Lloyd, this will only take a minute and I won't have to bug you and you won't have to dodge me. How about it? Can you give me one minute?"

"I'll give you exactly sixty seconds."

Fifteen minutes later, I hung up the phone and wrote a $300 order. From that day until I stopped calling on him six years later, he never failed to start each conversation with the words, "I'm busy, call me later." I never failed to reply, "This will only take a minute." He became a very good, twice-a-month customer.

CHECKLIST FOR AFTER THE SALE

- ❏ Record callback information
- ❏ Fill out CIF card
- ❏ Complete order sheet
- ❏ Address envelopes for any mail-outs customer requested
- ❏ Refile CIF into proper cycle

While these tasks may seem simple and not to require a checklist, you will be amazed how quickly confusion sets in when all the paperwork is not done at once. I have seen the wrong merchandise sent to the wrong customer. I know of cases when a customer was ready to buy, but the salesman didn't jot down the time he was to call back, thus losing that sale and all subsequent sales forever. I have failed to write down a new buyer's name on a CIF card because I was sure I would remember it an hour later. Save time, save embarrassment. Do everything in the order that it is supposed to be done. You will be glad you did.

IN PARTING . . .

Never intentionally be rude to a buyer. Because we are dealing with people over the telephone, we can never be sure of the situation at the other end. A burned bridge cannot be recrossed. If you just cannot seem to make a convert out of a prospect, move on to the next one, and do not look back.

There is no such thing as a wasted call. We learn from each person we talk to. In time, our intuition takes over, and with each passing day, you will find yourself stronger and wiser.

eight

Is It Possible to Push Too Hard?

What about Bob Fields? When last we checked, he still had not given Hector an order. Is he going to, or is he just wasting Hector's time? The only thing certain about a customer who tells you to call back is that at least he is not rude enough to tell you to go fly a kite. No sale is a sale until it is written. Bob still needs some work, but there is a fine line between persuasion and pressure. I have mentioned this elsewhere in this book, but it bears repeating: *you cannot browbeat a customer into giving you an order.* You can push a bill of goods down the buyer's throat only once, and sometimes, not even once.

THE DANGERS IN PRESSURE SELLING

Worse than not making a quota is trying to explain to the sales manager why an order you booked was returned unclaimed. You not only have a charge-back to your sales quota, but you have cost the company unnecessary freight, complicated bookkeeping procedures, and created a boondoggle in shipping. Why? You forced an issue. In this situation, no one wins. The telemarketer doesn't because the customer will probably not accept his calls in the future. The customer lost, because every avenue of merchandise is important. The company lost because it will not get a second chance to overcome the stigma created by the telemarketer's actions. It is a situation that can occur with the best of us, despite our best intentions.

How can this be avoided? Step one is to *never* book an order you think is not going to fly! This is perhaps one of the hardest aspects of telemarketing. With managers on our backs, demanding that quotas be met, financial demands seem to never lighten. And, with a world full of hostile customers (at least, sometimes it seems they are all hostile), the temptation to look the other way when a deal seems weak is overwhelming. I have yielded to this temptation myself, and almost without exception, each time I have succumbed, I have come to regret it.

By a deal "not flying," I mean the feeling we instinctively develop that tells us the buyer on the other end of the line has no intention of accepting the merchandise when it arrives or, if he does, he will not be able or perhaps even willing to pay for it. Not your problem, you say? You're there to sell it, someone else is there to collect for it. Wrong! How long do you think you will have your job when your sales manager has to clean up after you, making things right? Once, maybe twice, but after that, it is going to get old. I have sat on both sides of the desk—that of the salesman and that of the manager. What I'm saying is this: *A bogus sale is not worthy of a professional telemarketer.* Remember, respect begins with your position and from there moves upward. So should you.

Not every sale that turns sour will be your fault. A buyer is a human being, contrary to the way many of them choose to portray themselves. They have the same pressures on them as we have on us. Let's try to analyze this situation from a purely objective viewpoint. For the next few pages, we are going to be unbiased, impartial judges. Let's see how this looks from both sides.

WHEN IS THE SITUATION HOPELESS?

Hector called Bob Fields four times. Each time he gets a different reason why Bob is not ready to buy. With each excuse, Bob makes another promise, leaves enough room for doubt. Hector all the while still believes an order is forthcoming. On the fifth call, Hector pinned Bob down to a firm commitment. Let's listen:

✪   TeleSell 22   ✪

Promises Made to Make the Sale

"I can probably use a few hundred of your authentic leather picture frames, but I don't need them until next week."

"Tell you what, Bob. These little babies are going fast, and by next week I'm afraid we'll be out of them. Why don't I write them up for you now and hold the shipment until Monday afternoon? That way, you can be sure you've got them coming at the sale price, but they won't actually be in your warehouse until the following Monday. Sound okay to you?"

"You won't release them until Monday?"

"No problem. Now then, how many dozen?"

I won't bore you with the details of what happened next, as you can probably figure out the story. Thursday afternoon, just before the pay period came to an end, Hector realized he was $2,000 off his quota. Looking in his drawer, he saw the order for Bob's authentic leather picture frames and figured, why not, it's close enough to Monday to release the shipment. After all, the man did order them. Hector figured it wouldn't hurt to let them ship a few days early.

The order was turned into Hector's manager, the warm-hearted Ernie Chill, who, while amazed that Hector was able to unload 1,200 picture frames to a new customer, was nevertheless eager to make his quota too. He passed the order on to processing. Processing, in an unusual fit of efficiency, got the order down to shipping before close of business that same day. Shipping took the order to be a message from God and packed the twenty-four crates the same afternoon. They didn't sit on the dock more than twenty minutes when an enterprising expediter saw a chance to load them on a common carrier waiting to pick up another load. This shipment just broke a company record for dispatch. All would have been fine, except over the weekend, Bob realized that now was not the time to run a sale on leather picture frames—especially since he discovered twenty-five cases of them sitting in a forgotten basement storeroom.

No problem. He'd just call his friend Hector and explain the whole thing. Call off the order and buy something else next week. Too late! By the time Bob got hold of Hector, those little devils were already halfway across Montana . . . heading for Bob's store. What! They weren't supposed to be shipped until today. The order was not even supposed to be processed until late in the day, and now, because of some overeager salesman, Bob would have to explain to 'his boss why he ordered billions more of a product of which they had already cornered the market and had a plentiful supply.

Bob's solution? Refuse the shipment. If it comes down to Bob looking bad or Hector having to eat the freight on this order, there is no contest. Salesmen come and go, but to Bob, his job is worth protecting. The end result of this debacle has Hector explaining to Ernie why he jumped the gun on this order and explaining to Bob why the shipment left early. In addition to this, he is probably going to have to write off the time and money he invested trying to develop Bob into a viable customer.

LOSING CREDIBILITY WITH YOUR COMPANY AND YOUR CUSTOMER

So what has happened here? Hector made his quota on Thursday, and one short week later, he's doing a tap dance on Ernie's desk, trying to explain what a nerd Bob is for not accepting the merchandise he ordered. Bob is mad at both Big Bang and Hector. Big Bang is not sure if Bob is a flake or if Hector is a con artist, but in either case, the damage Hector has done between the two companies borders on irreparable. Bob is labeled a nut, Hector is viewed with suspicion. All because he succumbed to the temptation of rushing an order to make his quota.

If this is the first time it has happened, Hector may get off with a stern lecture and a warning. If it has happened before, Hector had best get out the classified section of the newspaper and start checking "Jobs Wanted."

What a different scenario this would have been if Hector had leveled with Ernie. Ernie is a reasonable boss. He wanted to make quota as badly as Hector did. He would have picked up the phone, called Bob, and worked out the whole problem. Then, if Bob got a terminal case of buyer's remorse the following Monday, at least Hector would have been in the clear. Instead, he may now have to clear out his desk.

I do not mean to preach, but I tell you from experience, *no good can come from a bogus sale.* None! Actions such as Hector's make it harder for all telephone solicitors to make a living.

STRIKING A BALANCE BETWEEN SUPPLY AND DEMAND

There is an inherent fact about telemarketing: *the sale is more important to the seller than to the buyer.* There are many reasons for this, but primarily it is because there are more sellers than buyers. Rarely have I seen a situation where the customer needed me more than I needed him. There are times, such as when a particular industry is in the throes of a shortage (for instance, batteries for electronic games during Christmas), when it appears to be a seller's market. But this is illusionary at best. Sure, the company that has an ample supply of batteries may appear to rest comfortably in the catbird seat, but it is clearly a situation which will remedy itself in time.

When the shortage is over and the pipelines are full, the buyer who was made to feel at the mercy of a particular salesman will exact his revenge. He will place his orders elsewhere, and the guy who squeezed first will be squeezed last.

During the citizens band radio boom in the mid-seventies, I worked for a company able to get its hands on a particularly scarce piece of merchandise. In fact, we had a lock on the entire production of this item. The sales manager of our firm came up with what he considered to be a concept so brilliant, he fully expected to be interviewed by *The Wall Street Journal.* He placed an allocation embargo on this product, restricting its sale to one unit for each fifty dollars worth of other merchandise ordered. Our customers bristled at this high-handed attitude, but our boss just smiled and said, "We're the only game in town. If they want our product, they'll sit at our table."

He was right. They grumbled, they cursed, but ultimately they met our requirements. Strangely enough, as soon as a competitor of ours found another source for this item and offered it to our customers without strings, we not only lost our market share in that item, but it was only a matter of time before we faced bankruptcy.

The point is this. If we have something to sell, so does somebody else. As soon as the second party makes it known that he has what we have, the dance is over and the work begins. We do not own our customers. We borrow them and try to take good care of them so we can continue to enjoy the use of them. But, I promise you, we can no more count on absolute customer loyalty than we can fly. Treat them well, and chances are, they might stay with us. Treat them badly, and almost certainly lose them.

THE ADVANTAGES OF HONEST DEALING

If we cannot hold a customer without bending his arm occasionally, how can we hold him? *The best way to get and keep a customer is through honest efforts.* You say the company you work for does not believe in honesty? Then I say, hit the road and find one that does. Without a moment's hesitation, I say to you, integrity builds a territory. Nothing else will last. From the first grade on, we have all been told, a house cannot be built without a firm foundation. Truer words were never written!

What are honest efforts? First and foremost, it is knowing your customer—knowing him well. This includes things such as his age bracket, marital status, race, creed, and military service history. His level of education, his taste in music, in humor, even in members of the opposite sex are all composite parts of your customer's makeup. Why is any of this important to a sales effort? The answer can be found in the basic study of human nature.

THE PROPER USE OF THE CUSTOMER'S NAME

We were all given a name shortly after birth. Some of us were given really great names, names like Rip or Sebastian, David or John. Some of us were given names which forevermore will cause us to fight the urge to hunt our parents down and exact vengeance. But the important thing is, we were all named something. No matter what we think of our names, we all like to hear them pronounced aloud. When we speak to our friends, we use their names in our conversation with them. Think of the last time you had an intimate conversation with your significant other. At least once every twenty sentences or so, you spoke his or her name. Why? It gave further intimacy to an already intimate conversation.

How much better it is to use our customers' names when addressing them! But, be careful. Too many references to his name, and it sounds like you are reading a script. Thus, one of the best ways to warm up a prospect and, at the same time, make him unaware of the warming process, is to sprinkle his favorite word into the conversation—and that word happens to be his name. A word of caution here. If a customer were to introduce himself as Lawrence, or herself as Margaret, do not begin your relationship with him or her by using the familiar Larry or Maggie. If they preferred those pet names, rest assured you would have been the first to know. We tend to confuse intimate verbiage with true intimacy. They are not the same!

A buyer for a large wholesale house in Utah was on my call list for three months. I knew he was a heavy hitter, but I could not manage to sustain a conversation with him for more then a few minutes. His name was Will Torrence, and when he answered the phone, he would always say, "Will, here." Invariably, I would begin the conversation by saying, "Will, this is your friend, Phillip."

Shortly afterwards, he would be gone, sometimes giving me an order, sometimes not, but always with a briskness reserved for someone you really don't want to talk with. Finally, I asked my sales manager if he had any clue to what the problem was. He listened in on my next call to Will. Afterwards I asked him if he knew what I was doing wrong.

"Yep," he answered. "You called yourself by your proper given name but called him by a nickname. By doing that, you were saying to him that you're his better, and he doesn't like you for it!"

How stupid, I thought! That could not be it. Or could it? The next time I called, I began the conversation by saying, "William, this is your friend, Phillip." Bingo! I hit the mark dead center. His response was forty degrees warmer then it had been before. He even told me a joke. He was like a different man on the phone. And why? Because I zeroed in on a prejudice that even Will did not know he possessed. He did not like to be called "Will"! It was that simple. He preferred to be called William, yet everyone, including himself, referred to him as "Will." From that day, every time we spoke, it was "William" and "Phillip." To this day, he is a great customer!

Each buyer is different, yet each is basically the same. If a telemarketer were to call fifty buyers in one day, each would be basically the same as the last, yet each one would possess enough differences that it would make them seem like they were from fifty different planets. Each buyer has pressure on him to perform. He must buy items that sell at competitive prices. He must schedule enough of the product to arrive at his location in time to meet the selling season for that item and have exactly enough inventory to satisfy the demands of a very fickle public. At the same time, he cannot have leftover stock taking up space when the product stops selling. And we thought our job was tough!

Given these circumstances, it is no wonder there is so much resistance to the phone salesman. In fact, it is a wonder we write any orders at all! There are things we can do, however, to help the buyer suspend his doubts and fears, at least momentarily, and allow him to listen to what we have to say. Remember, just as you would not grab a saddle and run for a horse not yet broken, you should never attempt to overwhelm a new customer with facts and figures out of the blue to try and force an order out of him. It does happen, but it occurs so rarely that when it does occur, I am always skeptical of the righteousness of the order. I almost always smell a rat when a buyer seems too eager to buy!

IN PARTING . . .

The basic concept to grasp here is that most buyers already have suppliers, vendors, and wholesalers filling their merchandise needs. Many of these vendors have been servicing them for years, often decades. What would make a man who is content with his current suppliers turn to you? Nothing! Nothing except better service, better prices, a better quality of goods, or most importantly, a better relationship.

nine

How to Find
New Customers

Up to now I have dealt with how to treat a customer once he has been found. This chapter deals with how to find him. Depending on your product, there are dozens of ways to ferret out the elusive "great customer." Some are obvious, some less so. But no matter how good a salesman you are, nothing can be done until you locate someone to sell. I have started with the easiest and most conventional approaches, and by the time you finish this chapter, you will be ready to offer your services to the CIA.

ASK: WHO DO YOU KNOW?

Three times a year, Hector reviews his customer list for buyers who are the most receptive and friendly. He makes a notation on their CIF cards to ask a question when next he speaks to them. The question is simple: "Who do you know that I should know?" The answers to this question

93

will assist in the expansion of his customer base. The conversation would go like this:

Ⓒ   *TeleSell 23*   Ⓒ

Who Do You Know?

"Thanks for the order, Pat. I'll get it out to you in the morning."

"No problem, Hector. Bye, now."

"Oh, Pat. I need to ask you something before we hang up."

"Shoot."

"Who do you know that I should know in our line of sales? I don't mean someone in direct competition with you, but someone you may know who would benefit from doing business with me. Maybe someone you met at a convention, or a buyers' show?"

"Well, let me think. Do you know Martin Bowers over in Kingsport?"

"No, I don't think so. What kind of a store does he have?"

"Like mine, only a little bigger. He's a pretty good old boy. He could use the stuff you sell."

"Great, I'll give him a call. What's the name of his store?"

"Just a sec, I've got his card some place. Here it is. Bowers's Appliances and Television. His name is Martin Bowers. His phone is 555-1889. Give him a call."

"And it won't affect you if I sell to him?"

"Oh, no. He's sixty miles down the road. Besides, we swap merchandise all the time. He was in here just last week. Call him."

"I will. Thanks for the lead, and thanks for the order."

As soon as he has a dial tone, Hector's fingers are dialing the number Pat gave him. When the number answers, the conversation will go like this:

℃   TeleSell 24   ℃

Leads from "Who Do You Know?" (Part 1)

Ring . . . Ring . . . Ring.

"Bowers's Appliances, may I help you?"
"Martin Bowers, please."
"May I tell him who's calling?"
"Sure, this is Hector Holt. I'm a friend of Pat Wallace."

STOP

What is happening here? Hector called a man he does not know, identified himself as a friend of a person he does business with, and is about to be put right through to a prospective new buyer. Will Martin take the call? Bet the farm!

℃   TeleSell 25   ℃

Leads from "Who Do You Know?" (Part 2)

"Martin Bowers speaking. Can I help you?"
"Mr. Bowers, Pat Wallace, in Winnsboro, suggested I call you. My name is Hector Holt, and I'm with the Big Bang Novelty Company. I've known Pat for quite a while, and today, while he was placing an order with me, he suggested you would be the ideal person for me to get to know. He said you had a bigger store than his and that you're a good old boy."

"Well, Pat's been known to stretch the truth a bit. How can I help you?"

ESTABLISHING A SECOND-PARTY RELATIONSHIP

It is only a matter of time before Hector and Martin become close business associates. Hector was able to establish an immediate intimacy with Martin, based not on what the two men felt toward each other, but rather on the mutual association both men had with the third party, Pat Wallace. This is a big step. The situation here is the same as if Hector was asking a stranger for a date. She might say yes, she might say no. But, if a friend of Hector's introduced him to the woman, the odds are better than even that he would at least get the chance to talk to her.

It is the same principle here. Martin took the phone call, not because he wanted to talk to a stranger named Hector Holt, but rather because the name Pat Wallace was mentioned. Pat was a friend of Martin's, ergo, any friend of Pat's is a friend of . . .

Hector did not lie to Martin. Far from it, he told the complete truth. Pat did indeed ask Hector to call Martin. He said Martin's store was larger, and he said Martin was a good old boy. All Hector did was assume an air of familiarity, and this is, in and of itself, no violation of ethics or proper business conduct. If Martin read more into this than there was, it certainly was through no fault of Hector's.

The referral system is not new. Salespeople have used it for years. The telephone, however, has made it possible to find a lead and be speaking to that prospect within a few minutes. It does not matter where the other prospect is: Walla Walla, Washington, or Key Largo, Florida. Hector, through the use of the telephone, will have him in his sights within minutes.

The most obvious advantage of a "who do you know" program is simply that it saves time. Had Hector stumbled upon Martin on his own, he would have invested several phone calls and a good deal of effort just to arrive at the place he started. These efforts were alleviated thanks to his friend Pat. Hector simply took a running jump to ascend the first few rungs up the ladder in writing an order.

The only down side to this approach is that Hector must be careful not to ask the "who do you know" question too often. If he continues to go back to Pat Wallace with more requests for assistance, Pat will soon grow tired of having his Christmas card list raided. Hector should be sure to thank Pat for his suggestions. If Pat has another prospect for Hector, he will bring it forward on his own. Four months from now, however, when Hector dusts off his list of newly made clients, you can be assured he will ask Martin, "Who do you know?"

THE PROS AND CONS OF LIST BUYING

For every industry in America, for every financial endeavor, for every group bound together by a common reason, there is a list of names available for purchase. These lists identify the who, where, and how-to-reach of any portion of these people. In short, if a need exists to contact any group, so does a list. Now the question arises: is buying a list a reasonable way to find prospective customers? There are many factors to consider before this question can be answered.

The bottom line for any list acquisition is easy to comprehend. Will the purchase of this list add significantly to the total sales effort of the organization? When I started my own sales company, I was overwhelmed by the prospect of merely paying someone ten cents to tell me the name of a company, its address, its phone number, and in many cases, the owner or buyer for that company. I clearly remember thinking, *this is too good!* It cannot be this easy.

It wasn't. The list contained 1,000 names of television and radio dealers in a six-state area. For this treasure, I paid $100. Page after page of names, addresses, contacts, and phone numbers neatly piled on my desk. I gleefully rubbed my hands together. A piece of cake. All I needed do was call these names, offer my wares, and I would be rich. I dialed the number of the first prospect.

His phone had been disconnected! His and four more out of the first twelve names. Of the seven remaining on the first page, two had electronic answering machines, one had a live answering service, and one was about to retire. This left me three names that resulted eventually in one sale. Sounds terrible, doesn't it? But, one out of twelve was better than none out of twelve, and finally, three months later, my sales team had worked all 1,000 names. We ended up with about sixty new customers. Did I waste my money? I don't think so. Did I waste my time? Definitely!

The problem with lists is that they tend to grow old. Inasmuch as they are sold by the name, the owners of such lists have little incentive to weed out the deadwood. They tell you in advance that a percentage of the names will not be viable. Most list sellers will claim the deadwood to be approximately five percent. I would venture to say it's closer to fifteen. Still, even at that, one good customer can pay for the entire list. There is no denying the validity of the concept; the problem comes in the execution of the list.

WHEN TO HIRE A QUALIFIER

I found a solution to this dilemma. I always hire a "bird dog" to work any list I acquire. I give them the title of "qualifier." This person's sole responsibility is to call each name on the list, determine whether the prospect is credible (that is to say, worth pursuing), and inquire as to the degree of interest each prospect has. If requested to do so, the qualifier will mail the prospect a catalog. They create CIF cards on the prospects requesting catalogs. The CIF cards are divided among my sales team, and those names are again worked after the prospective buyers have had an opportunity to receive and read the catalog.

The basic quality a qualifier must possess is the ability to listen. I feel that women make better qualifiers than men for this very reason. By nature, women are more attuned to other people. They possess an inquisitive nature, yet in a manner that will allow probing into the inner mind of a prospect without running the risk of offending the prospect. Put a woman in this position, particularly if you are in a male-dominated industry. Men will tell a woman they just met things they will not tell their brothers! I do not know the psychological reasoning behind this, but it is true. Every time I have hired a qualifier, I have hired a woman. They are best suited for this particular task. Since the bulk of a qualifier's information comes from auditory input, it makes firm business sense to put a person in this post who was born with the ability to hear not only what is said, but what is not.

Using a qualifier has many advantages. Primarily, it saves time. By using a qualifier to eliminate the deadwood and find the true prospective clients, my sales force did not develop an "attitude" about the list. If they experienced the defeat and rejection my qualifier had, they would soon have given up on the list itself. By allowing a trained professional to handle this laborious project, I was in effect telling my salespeople that they were too valuable to use on such a menial task. And they were!

A subsidiary advantage to qualifying the list is in saved postage, catalogs, and office supplies. A qualifier does not have a personal agenda. They will only send out catalogs to clients who seem viable. Unlike a professional telemarketer, who soon realizes the direct link between literature out, sales in, the qualifier will send literature only to those people who are really interested. This tends to make the CIF cards they create more substantial and valuable. Qualifiers can be taught to eliminate deadwood, but more importantly, they can be taught to recognize a diamond in the rough.

A third reason to use qualifiers is that they will be in a posture to elicit the most information from a prospective customer. They tell the prospective client up front that they are not salespeople. They identify themselves and their company and explain that they are only interested in ascertaining whether or not the prospect is interested in receiving literature from their company. Qualifiers should work with CIF cards in front of them. This will allow them to gain as much information as practical, as quickly and efficiently as possible.

Asking questions may well be the most difficult part of prospecting new customers. We are strangers, asking other strangers questions such as, "When do you get to work?" or "Are you a corporation or a sole proprietorship?" These questions need to be answered, but it is important they are asked in such a manner as not to offend the prospect. A good qualifier can do this. They can intersperse their questions with statements such as, "I really am sorry to take up your time; I know you're a busy person."

This is not an attitude a telemarketer can afford to adopt. Remember, your best business relationships will be based on mutual trust and respect. It is important the buyer realize your time is valuable also. To that end, when a salesman finally does call on the prospect for the first time, he can do so with the attitude of a sales specialist, not someone just looking for an order. The qualifier has already done the dirty work. The reason you know the buyer's name, his hours, and his buying cycles is that a skilled qualifier was able to put the buyer at ease long enough for him to answer the qualifier's questions.

In the beginning of this book, I mentioned that the buyer has no sensory input concerning you other than what your voice conveys. It is of the utmost importance the buyer realize that in your opinion you are no less important than he and that your time is just as important. Let the qualifier be humble and apologetic. The sales specialist must maintain a fine balance between friendliness and professionalism.

WHAT A QUALIFIER SHOULD KNOW

Be sure the qualifier understands her job. A qualifier is not a salesperson, although many of them can develop into first-rate telemarketers. The basic job of the qualifier is to separate the chaff from the wheat. They don't always get it right, they sometimes call wheat chaff and vice versa, but a good qualifier is right most of the time. They are able to spot the difference between someone killing time and a free decision maker.

What does your qualifier need to know? That is a book in itself, but there are some broad areas we can cover here. A good qualifier is a good listener. It is not necessary, nor is it even advisable to stress the technical side of your industry. For example, if you market products to auto parts dealers, your qualifier need not be conversant with the inner workings of an automatic transmission. What he or she does need to know is that your company carries an extensive line of parts and components to repair almost any transmission in use today. Remember, his or her function is to qualify, not to sell:

©   TeleSell 26   ©

Using a Qualifier

Ring . . . Ring . . . Ring.

"Woody's Transmissions, may I help you?"

"Mr. Woodruff, please."

"Just a minute."

"Woody, here."

"Mr. Woodruff, Anne Kenter. I'm with Build Em Good Transmission Exchange. We are a major distributor of quality auto parts. I'm calling to make sure you have our latest catalog."

"Build Em Good, eh? No. I don't believe I've got your book."

"Well, it's a good thing I called then. I'll get one in the mail for you today. Shall I mark it to your attention?"

"Might as well. No one else around here can read."

"I know that feeling. I swear we've got a guy in our mail room that only reads dead languages. I'll see that your name is entered on our list and send you out our latest catalog and sale flier."

"Sounds great."

"So that you'll know, we send out sale sheets each month around the twenty-fifth. Someone will follow them up a few days later with a quick call to see if there's anything you need from us."

"Is that going to be you?"

"No. I just send out catalogs. They won't let me do any selling. They think I'm just another pretty face."

"Well, tell them I said to let you do what you want."

"I sure will. Before I go, let me make sure I've got the right mailing address. You're located at 1412 North Rampart Turnpike, Suite 4?"

"Yep, that's us."

"Great. It was good talking to you, Mr. Woodruff, and thanks for your time."

"No problem."

"By the way, what's the best time of day for our salesman to call you?"

"Any time after ten in the morning. I'm usually covered up with estimates until then."

"Oh, I see. You do a lot of transmission repairs?"

"I don't know what *you* call a lot, but we rebuild about twenty-five to thirty-five units each week."

"My goodness! You are a busy man."

"Well, I don't do them myself, I've got six mechanics on line. But yeah, we do a right smart business here."

"That's really impressive! Again, thanks for your time, and be looking for our catalog. You ought to receive it in the next three or four days."

"I'll keep a look out for it."

"Bye, now."

CONVERTING THE QUALIFIED PROSPECT INTO A BONA FIDE CUSTOMER

That was a great prospecting call. Woody will not be surprised when he receives the newest edition of Build Em Good's catalog. Nor will he be surprised to receive his first phone contact next week from a telemarketer concerning his inventory needs. In fact, thanks to the skillful techniques Anne used, Woody is already beginning to equate Build Em Good with a personality. Heretofore, even if he was familiar with the reputation of Build Em Good, it was just a faceless, voiceless warehouse somewhere in the Midwest. Now, and until his first contact with someone from the telemarketing program, Build Em Good is a nice-sounding young woman with a sense of humor and an understanding of some of the problems he faces every day.

What are some of the techniques Anne used to elicit information from Woody? For starters, she was smooth and easy in her conversation. She did not press him for information; in fact, most of what she learned about his operation was volunteered by the prospect himself! She also used what I call the "PS" method. The PS method works in telemarketing just as it does in letters. Remember, she had already said good-bye to Woody, when she said, "Oh, by the way." From that point on, she was able to determine the best calling time for him, how he spent his mornings, how many transmissions he repairs daily, how many mechanics he has employed, and how business is right now. Not bad for a conversation that was all but over!

What did Anne find that will help her qualify Woody as a good prospect? For starters, she found him to be re-. ceptive to talking to a stranger on the phone. She also managed to ascertain that the man was in charge of at least a six-bay garage, determined by the fact he has six mechanics on his payroll. She would alert the telemarketer who works this account not to call before ten in the morning. As a personal aside, she can note on his CIF card that Woody has a sense of humor. (It is my belief that a man with a sense of humor makes a better customer then one without.)

Her overall impression of Woody was good. She will address a catalog to him and staple the business card of the telemarketer who will handle Woody's account to the front of the catalog. She will also include the specials sheet for this month. After this is done, she will pass the CIF card on to the sales manager, or if her organization uses a "next up" system, she will give it to the telemarketer next in line for a prospect.

This system gives the telemarketer a head start on the sales process. When the telemarketer handling this account, Richard Lyles, called Woody the next week, the call went like this:

ℂ   *TeleSell 27*   ℂ

Following Up on the Qualifier

Ring . . . Ring . . . Ring.

"Woody's Transmissions, may I help you?"

"Woody, please."

"Speaking."

"Woody, this is Richard Lyles with the Build Em Good Transmission Exchange. Anne spoke to you last week and sent you our catalog along with our monthly specials sheet. I'm just following up, making sure you got it."

"Yep, got it last Friday. Haven't had a chance to look it over yet. But I got it."

"Great. Got any questions about our company I could answer for you?"

"Well, yeah. I was wondering . . ."

This call will be infinitely easier than it would have been if it had been made cold. The transition from total stranger to business acquaintance was made easier by the fact that Anne had paved the way. I cannot emphasize enough: a good qualifier is worth his or her weight in orders.

FINDING LEADS WHERE YOU LEAST EXPECT THEM

Today, Hector is looking for ways to break Ernie's record of new customers found in a single month. He has already employed a "who do you know" drive, and there are no more lead cards or coupons to exploit. In short, Hector is on his own and must explore new horizons. Before he and his team of telemarketers can sell more products, they must first find and identify new markets. This is the fun part of telemarketing. You will be impressed with Hector's ingenuity!

On his way to work this morning, Hector read a national daily newspaper. Let's call it *America Today*. While reading the section listing some of the local events in different states across America, he noticed a rather interesting item. Jacksonville, Texas, had a tomato festival over the weekend. Part of the festivities included a tomato "chucking" contest. Participants in this activity would divide into two camps. Each camp would spend fifteen minutes pelting the other team with overly ripe tomatoes. There were other activities also, such as a contest to judge which local citizen grew a tomato that most closely resembled Willie Nelson. All activities in the festival revolved around the production and promotion of tomatoes. These people took their tomatoes seriously!

Of what possible interest could this be to Hector? Big Bang Novelty was built on odd items and weird knickknacks. Big Bang has in its warehouse wooden tomato salt and pepper shakers, ceramic tomato sugar bowls, tomato-shaped casserole dishes, even tomato-decorated hand towels. A match made in heaven! Hector found a city filled with tomato-crazed citizens, and he was sitting on top of a warehouse full of tomato-related novelties.

The only thing standing between Hector and the telemarketing hall of fame was the fact that Big Bang did not have a single customer in the city of Jacksonville. Hector did not even know where Jacksonville, Texas, was located. No problem, the phone company would know. As soon as he hit his office, Hector was on the phone, calling his friendly AT&T operator. Soon, he knew Jacksonville was in the 214 area. Now, he needed only to find a customer there.

In checking his customer list in the aforementioned area code, Hector found a number of clients located within that area. Most were in Dallas, some in smaller cities in the area, but none in the city of Jacksonville itself. Being unfamiliar with the actual geographic location of the city would be a handicap in locating a prospective customer. Hector needs a friend in Jacksonville to steer him toward a prospective customer. But who? Who in Jacksonville would have a reason to see Hector succeed in selling to a local merchant?

MAKING USE OF DIRECTORY ASSISTANCE

Picking up the phone, Hector called directory assistance in Jacksonville. He asked for the number of the public library. From the librarian he learned the name and phone numbers of the local newspaper, as well as the radio and television stations. Armed with this information, Hector's next call was to the advertising manager of the local newspaper.

© *TeleSell 28* ©

Friendly Leads (Part 1)

Ring . . . Ring . . . Ring.

"World Tribune and Local Gossip, may I help you?"

"Who's your advertising manager?"

"That would be Mr. Jacobs."

"Could you connect me, please?"

"Advertising, Jacobs speaking."

"Mr. Jacobs, my name is Hector Holt. I'm sales manager for Big Bang Novelty in New York, and I really need your assistance."

"Yes, Mr. Holt. What can I do for you?"

"Our company markets a large number of tomato-related novelties. I have some co-op advertising dollars to spend in your area, but I don't have the first clue as to who in your trade area I need to contact to move our product. I thought perhaps you might have some suggestions as to who I might call. In return for your help, I'll try to push the advertising to your paper, rather than radio. Any ideas?"

STOP

There are a few points I need to clear up. First, as much as he would like to, Hector does not really have any co-op money to spend. Second, while this is obviously not a truthful approach, in a more perfect world Hector would not have to supply an incentive for Mr. Jacobs to help him find a customer. Unfortunately, this is not a perfect world, and the only thing that will motivate Jacobs is the promise of additional advertising dollars for his paper. Last, ten minutes after Hector hangs up the phone, Jacobs will forget he ever spoke to anyone from Big Bang. That's human nature. Let's go back to the phone.

☏ *TeleSell 29* ☏

Friendly Leads (Part 2)

". . . rather than radio. Any ideas?"

"Novelty stores, huh. Let's see. How about Glen's Books and Gags? They've got a store in the mall, and one whole section is devoted to knickknacks and such. You might try them."

"Do you know the buyer's name, by chance?"

"Well, Kyle Henley owns the place. I guess you'd have to talk to him. Or his wife, Margaret. Either one of them could probably help you."

"Listen, you've been a big help. I'll certainly try to aim some business your way."

"No problem. Have a nice day."

"You, too."

One of the nicest things about small towns is that everybody knows everybody. There is no doubt in my mind that the director of advertising sales in any small town newspaper or radio station knows the owners of every small business within fifty miles. He would die before he shared that information with another advertising salesman, but if there is the possibility of increasing his advertising bookings, he will roll out the store. After Hector gets the phone number for the bookstore from directory assistance, the call will start like this:

ℭ   TeleSell 30   ℭ

Following Up on Friendly Leads

Ring . . . Ring . . . Ring.

"Glen's Books and Gags, may I help you?"

"Kyle Henley, please."

"This is Kyle."

"Kyle, my name is Hector Holt, and I'm with Big Bang Novelty, in New York. I read in *America Today* about the tomato festival there in Jacksonville. I think I might have a line of products that would prove profitable to you. I'd like to send you a catalog and price sheets."

"Sure, send them on."

"Great. I'll need your mailing address."

Bang! Another prospect added to the ever-growing list of Hector's clients. This is only one of many ways to ferret out customers who might otherwise never be found. There are many other methods.

USING COMMUNITY RESOURCES TO FIND PROSPECTS

Most cities have a Chamber of Commerce. This organization exists for the benefit of its members and for the growth of its city. It can be a strong tool for the telemarketer in search of a new market. I have used local police departments, fire departments, even churches to find new customers. The trick is to ask for a particular office, usually someone in public relations, often someone who would be in charge of dispatching services. Local delivery services, freight companies, taxicab dispatchers, even the postal service can assist in the search for a prospect who is likely to become a customer. Most of these people could not aid you in their official capacity. Their job description does not include giving out information to strangers over the phone. But if approached with an honest question, such as who in their city might sell the particular products you are selling, most of these people will be more than willing to share this information.

There are three things to remember when using this approach: (1) Be brief. Don't put a burden on these "bird dogs." If they are kind enough to help you without a financial reward, be gracious enough to conserve their time. (2) There is no reason to lie about your motive for calling. Tell them up front that you are a salesman with the XYZ Company and that you are looking for someone locally that might be a prospect for your wares. They will either help you or not, and if not there is always someone else. (3) This concept will not work in a metropolitan area. To be effective, you must be dealing with a small city or town and, even then, be prepared for rejection. The perfect size community for tapping into local resources is between

4,000 and 10,000 in population. More than 10,000 and the community becomes too large for any one person to have a firm handle on the comings and goings of the local business community. Less than 4,000 and the retail customer base will probably be too small to support a wholesale effort on your part.

Anyone can help. In any city of less than 10,000 there are always people who know everything that goes on in their community. The point is, every small town in America is essentially like any other. If you know what buttons to push, the whole plan comes together.

What we are essentially looking for is someone who would be familiar with the business community, as well as someone who would not mind talking about the activities in his or her city. I am not advocating doing anything more than just asking for directions. People want to help. They also want to feel important. In short, they will trip over themselves for an opportunity to tell a perfect stranger whom he should contact to sell his products.

Make use of special contacts or fraternal organizations of which you are a member. If you are a Rotarian, and you want to find someone to handle the combination umbrella -pencil sharpener your company has developed, don't hesitate to call the president of the Rotary Club in the city in which you are seeking a dealer. Tell him up front who you are and what you need.

There is a special benefit to using connections. Suppose you are a member of the Knights of Columbus. Find the local chapter of the KCs, and through them find a contact to help you obtain information about their city. Hector found a man named Hank Gettings. He asked Hank, "Who in your area would be a likely prospect for my product?" Hank directed Hector to Bill Morgan. Bill did indeed become a customer.

When Hector got Bill on the phone, the first words out of his mouth were, "Bill, I was talking to Hank Gettings earlier today, and he suggested I contact you. My name is Hector Holt with Big Bang Novelty, and I have a product that will allow you to bring in additional profit at a very nominal cost."

Now the fact that Hector knew a local guy, namely his newfound friend Hank Gettings, and the fact Hector knew Bill Morgan's name, put him two steps up on any other phone salesman that would call Bill today. *Note, Hector did not claim to have an endorsement from Hank, and he didn't dwell on any special affiliation he enjoyed as Hank's acquaintance!* All he needed was to flavor the conversation so it appeared that Hector was not without certain connections in Bill's community. There is nothing unethical or underhanded about this. He stated only the facts.

But what if you have no list of friends or acquaintances from which to draw? There are still ways to network an area in such a manner as to connect with a dealer or a new prospect. Consider your product. What is it you have to sell, and who buys it? Let's go back to Hector's warehouse. On a back shelf Hector discovers that Big Bang once made a huge purchase of solar-powered can openers and never ran a promotion on these items. Hector considered running them on special, then realized that this is exactly the type of thing he needed to spearhead a new customer drive. First, he must isolate the market; he will then match the market to the product.

ANALYZE YOUR PRODUCT—RESEARCH YOUR MARKET

Who would use a solar-powered can opener? For that matter, who buys any can openers? Obviously, someone who opens cans is the answer. But solar-powered? This would be used by someone either trying to conserve electricity or someone who did not have an electric outlet at their disposal. Campers! Right! Campers and people who spend a good deal of time outdoors. Hector continued his brainstorming. Where do people camp? Being a city boy, he ruled out Manhattan and Detroit. Colorado came to mind, as did Arizona, New Mexico, Texas, Oklahoma, Louisiana, and a multitude of southern states. Who sells camping supplies? Hardware stores, sporting goods stores, and several national department stores. Hector ruled out trying to sell them to Sears, which left his options limited to hardware stores and sporting goods stores.

All he needed now was a retail store which fell into one or both of the two targeted areas. Hector acquired an atlas which breaks states down by county and city. These are reasonable in price and can be found in most bookstores. For about the same amount of money as a ticket to the local cinema, he possessed all the geographic information he would ever need about any state in the union. An atlas such as this is essential for any national telemarketer.

Armed with his atlas, Hector was ready to explore new territories without ever leaving the confines of his office. He knew he wanted a city located in an area surrounded by open terrain, the type of area campers are likely to find inviting. Hector consulted the map and found a city which fit the profile he was seeking: Brighton, Colorado. Picking up his phone, he dialed directory information in Brighton. He asked for the number of Brighton Sporting Goods. There was no such listing. How about Brighton Hardware? Nope. Brighton Farm Supply? Nope. Brighton Ranch Supplies? Bingo! He called the number.

©   TeleSell 31   ©

Looking for Prospects

Ring . . . Ring . . . Ring.

"Brighton Ranch Supplies. Al, speaking."

"Al, do you sell camping supplies?"

"No, sure don't. You might try Camping Is Us, in the Green Market Square."

"Thanks, any place else in Brighton?"

"Well, Andy's Hardware sells some stuff, and of course, Greens Supply's got a right smart amount."

"Great, thanks for your help."

Hector now has three leads. Five minutes ago, all he had was an idea and 600 can openers. After getting the phone numbers from directory assistance, Hector made his calls. First, Camping Is Us:

©   TeleSell # 32   ©

Feeling Out the Territory (Part 1)

Ring . . . Ring . . . Ring.

"Camping Is Us, Gregg speaking."

"Gregg, who does the buying for your store?"

"We don't buy anything here. Everything comes out of our warehouse in Denver. You want that number?"

"Yeah, but I need to know, do you have any solar-powered can openers in stock?"

"Solar-powered?"

"Yeah."

"Never heard of such a thing."

"Okay. What's the number?"

Hector is not going to call the main office yet for several reasons. First, a company with a central buying office is not the usual customer for Big Bang. Remember, they deal with smaller operations. Secondly, the larger the customer, the slower they move. Hector wants to sell all

600 units today! Thirdly, if he does manage to cut a deal with the central buyer, he most likely will have to commit the total inventory to one chain. Such a sale would defeat the purpose of this promotion. Hector, you will remember, is on the prowl for new customers. He wants to include as many new prospects as he can to his potential customer list. He cannot do this if he sells all the product to one chain.

He will probably approach Camping Is Us at a later time, but now he is hunting for small but numerous customers, not one giant dealer. His next call? Andy's Hardware.

✪ *TeleSell 33* ✪

Feeling Out the Territory (Part 2)

Ring . . . Ring . . . Ring.

"Andy's, can I help you?"

"Who does the buying for your camping supplies?"

"That would be Mr. Hurley. Want to speak to him?"

"Please."

"Hurley, speaking."

"Mr. Hurley, my name is Hector Holt. I represent Big Bang Novelty in New York. I was talking to Al down at Brighton Ranch Supplies. He suggested that if I was looking for a dealer in Brighton to represent our line, your store would be one of the better choices. I've got a really **great** new item, one so new that not even Camping Is Us **has** it yet."

"Oh, yeah? Tell me about it."

Hector has found his market, and now he's pitching his product. If he scores here, he'll add a new customer to his list. If Hurley is not interested at this time, he'll place him on the prospect list. The next time Hector calls, he will know who to ask for, and Hurley will not be a stranger. If he totally strikes out, he has still got the third prospect to call, plus of course, if all else fails, he can pitch it to Camping Is Us. After he finishes his prospects in Brighton, he will repeat these same steps in other cities, and when he finishes in Colorado, he will go on to other states.

The point is: Hector does not know beans about the geography of Colorado. He knows even less about camping. But what he does know is how to sell on the phone, how to grab the competitive edge and make it work for him. Anyone who can sell, can sell anything on the telephone. And that's a fact!

HOW A TELEMARKETING PROGRAM CAN BENEFIT FROM ADVERTISING

There are many other ways to find prospects, including one of the most effective and time-tested: advertising. One of the most effective forms of advertising is print ads, placed in trade publications aimed at your industry. In these ads, always include a clip-out coupon, not the same as a postage-paid business reply card. This type of coupon has spaces provided for the name of the company, the buyer's name, and of course, address and phone. The coupon should be bordered by perforated lines. The top of the coupon should show your company's name, address, and a short line reading, "Please send me your latest catalog."

There is a very deep physiological motivation involved with this type of coupon, one which transcends the use of the prepaid card. A prepaid card takes only a moment to fill out and requires no special care, other than finding a mailbox. The clip-out coupon requires the prospective buyer to: (1) fill out information; (2) clip the coupon from the magazine; (3) address and put in an envelope; (4) place postage on the envelope; and (5) mail the request. If he has gone to this much bother, chances are he is somewhat serious about wanting to see literature concerning your product.

USING THE PREPAID BUSINESS REPLY CARD

I know all the arguments for the prepaid card. Printers love to print them because they cost more to make than a coupon ad, which is incorporated into the text of the magazine. The United States Postal Service loves them because each one placed in the mail is a guaranteed fee for them. Magazines love them because they convey a "trendy" concept to their readership. And sales managers like them because they are easier to stack and rubber band.

I *hate* them for two reasons. First, anything which requires no effort to use tends to be used by anyone with a few spare minutes on their hands. Sitting on a plane, waiting for dinner to be served, commuting on the train, or sifting through magazines in the doctor's office, these cards are just too great a temptation for the average person to fill out and mail. What a deal! Just write your address down on the back of a little card, drop it in at the next mailbox, and presto, you get a free catalog in a few days. When the catalog arrives, it really won't mean much. After all, it was easy enough to get. It is a safe bet that it receives less than priority treatment. Ralph Waldo Emerson stated it best when he said:

"That which we obtain too cheaply, we value not at all."

My second dislike for these prepaid cards is economic. Regardless of what is written on the back of the card, the person whose name appears as the addressee must, by contract, redeem each card for a few cents more than regular postcard postage. The one time I used this device, I paid for sixty cards that merely read, "No Thank You." Obviously these were sent back to us by people who held them in the same low esteem I do.

PROSPECTS FROM TRADE SHOWS

Another effective method of finding large numbers of new prospects is by attending trade shows. Not everyone will stop at your booth, but you will still receive a good amount of traffic. I have always placed a large, covered box, about twice the size of a hatbox, on the outer table of my displays. On the front of this box a sign reads simply:

Enter Our Free Drawing
Drop In Your Business Card
You Need Not Be Present To Win

At the end of each day's activities, I gather all the cards and place them in a large envelope. Making sure to date the envelope, I mark it to indicate the trade show it came from and the city. When I return to the office, at the conclusion of the show, I open each day's envelope one at a time. I record all the information from the cards on loose sheets of typing paper, being careful not to list more than ten prospects per sheet. I try to leave plenty of room for notes my qualifier will want to make on the sheet. After this is done, I return all the cards to a box and draw out a winning card. I make sure the winner receives his prize and make sure that he consents to having his name used in future advertisements.

Remember: *time is of the essence in sales*. When you employ this technique, make sure that your qualifier starts on these cards immediately. Let hime or her begin to contact the names you have gathered and ask them if they would like to have a catalog or other literature sent to them. These cards will not improve with age. Quite the contrary, the older they become, the less use they are.

Some time ago I decided to take up the sport of table billiards. I was moderately successful (beginner's luck), and the idea crossed my mind that perhaps my fortune would be made in the pool halls of America. I became engrossed in the game. It occurred to me that what I really needed was a $500 pool cue. With such a cue I was certain to become internationally famous. I called a national firm who manufactures such sticks and requested a catalog. Six months later it arrived in my morning mail. Six months!

Well, a lot happened in those six months. Most notable was the discussion I had with my wife about the amount of time I was spending in pool halls. After a great deal of soul-searching and one or two ultimatums thrown in by her, I decided that perhaps pool playing was better left to younger men. Or at least single ones.

The point of this narrative is: if the company had mailed me the catalog I requested when I requested it, I would have undoubtedly ordered the cue stick of my dreams. Six months later, when they did contact me, I was no longer in the market for such an item. They ultimately wasted not only their postage and their catalog, but they also wasted their time and lost a potential sale. It would have taken only a few moments to respond to my request. That few moments they neglected to spend cost them a $500 sale.

IN PARTING . . .

In telemarketing there are basically only two ways to increase sales. The first is through selling more product. The second is through finding more customers. There are many more intricate methods of finding new customers as well. The thing to remember is that there should be no bounds to your imagination. I have found customers by watching the news and hearing of an unusual event in a distant state which, with a little forethought, could be turned to my advantage. I have been tipped off to new accounts, I have followed buyers from job to job, I have even asked relatives and friends if they knew of anyone from their area who might have been interested in seeing the line of goods I sell.

I always take a small notebook with me whenever I'm on vacation and jot down the names and locations of businesses I see that might have been closed or that I could not work into my schedule right then and call them when I return to the office. The list of ways to develop new prospects is endless. Be ever-vigilant. Watch for and find new opportunities. Remember, every single customer on your list, *every single one,* began as a new account!

ten

Selling the Benefits

Every item you sell has two distinct aspects to its existence: features and benefits. Features are the physical aspects of the product, benefits are what makes things sell. Take an ordinary yellow pencil from your desk. When it was new, it was about seven inches long. It is about three-eights of an inch thick. It has a six-sided exterior, painted with an enamel finish. A wooden casing surrounds the lead in the center, and at the top of the pencil is a metal rim which holds a soft, pink eraser. On the side of the pencil is the legend "Made in America" and an Arabic numeral, probably a number two.

I have described the pencil in detail. If you had never seen one, you would now have a pretty good idea of what it looked like. But, if you had never seen one, would you know the purpose of all these features? Why is it seven inches long? Why the multisided, painted exterior? Why is it made of wood, not plastic or metal? What are the legends for, and what is the purpose of the eraser? Is the fact that the band holding the eraser in place is made of metal of any real importance?

THE DIFFERENCE BETWEEN BENEFITS AND FEATURES

We have all seen a pencil, and we can answer these questions for ourselves. But if I were trying to sell this item to someone who had never used one, I would begin by pointing out that the standard length of the instrument allows it to be used for a considerable period of time, thereby making its purchase a prudent one. Of course, I would first explain that it is a writing instrument. I would say that the beveling of the exterior inhibits the pencil's tendency to roll away from the user and onto the floor every time it is set down on a desk or table. I would point out that coating a pencil with a bright enamel finish helps keep fingerprints, dirt, and grime from making the pencil appear dirty. I would explain that the legend identifies the product's manufacturer, the place of origin, and the relative softness of the lead. The metal clasp which retains the eraser will allow the user to rub out any errors and keeps the pencil and eraser together.

Do you see the difference? At first I described only the features the pencil had to offer. There was nothing noteworthy about these features. Then I translated the features into benefits—the beveled surface that keeps the pencil from rolling off the desk for instance. I related to the potential buyer why the features are necessary and desirable. In short, features without benefits amount to nothing more than an exercise in futility. If I did not consider it important that my pencil remain where I set it, then it would not matter whether it had a beveled finish or a smooth, round exterior.

This example can be reworded to include every single item in your home or office. We buy a sweater because it is made of virgin wool. So what? Without knowing that virgin wool tends to be warmer than acrylic, the higher price of virgin wool sweaters would turn the customer off. We purchase a refrigerator because it is frost free. This is a nice feature. It becomes a benefit only when the salesman explains that never will we have to spend hours hacking out the ice which non–frost-free units accumulate on their interior walls. We will never have a mess to clean up because we now have a refrigerator which never needs to be defrosted.

Do not try to sell features. *Sell benefits!*

When we sell over the phone, features become even more ambiguous. Conversely, benefits become more important. When speaking to a customer about packaging, you might say to that buyer, "The item is packaged in a sturdy, attractive, four-color box which features a hang-up tab." This feature only becomes a benefit when you point out that the customer has two options of display, either on a gondola or on a peg rack. Now, armed with this knowledge, your buyer can see the benefit of this packaging. He is being given flexibility of display, a benefit which may well result in additional sales.

While it is not necessary for you to understand how the lead got into the pencil—something I still don't know—it is incumbent upon you to understand why this particular pencil is of superior design and engineering. You must be able to recognize the connection between features and benefits. There can be little doubt that a German sports car capable of going from zero to sixty in six seconds is a nice feature, but unless you are registered to run in the Indianapolis 500 next spring, this particular feature may never translate into a benefit.

PROBLEMS IN CONFLICTS OF PERCEPTION

In every product, there is a conflict of perception between utility and romance. Every product, be it copy paper or expensive diamonds, is vested with these two properties. There exists the purpose for which the product was manufactured and the motivation under which it is purchased. There is absolutely nothing wrong with romancing the product. In saying this, I wish to be crystal clear on one point. A great deal of difference exists between romancing an item, sometimes called product enhancement, and out-right lying. I have stated many times in this book, and I will state it again: *never lie about what you are selling!* Do not say something is genuine leather when it is really embossed vinyl.

I once sold an item that came packaged in a very attractive, leatherlike zippered case. I would invariably describe the case as *genuine imitation* leather. Most customers would snicker at this description, but it was honest. If I thought the buyer was under the impression that the case was genuine leather, I would repeat my statement. Usually, by at least the second round, he would understand what I was saying. The important thing here was to be sure that the customer understood that the case was *not* real leather. If he were to purchase the item in question and discover the case was plastic when expecting leather, the sale would not have stood. Moreover, the credibility which previously existed between the buyer and myself would have been destroyed.

There is a Jamaican proverb which seems to have been coined for telemarketers and buyers of telemarketed goods. "Fool me once, shame on you. Fool me twice, shame on me!" This is not to say you cannot use terms such as ". . . the look of real leather," or ". . . if I didn't know better, I'd think it was the real thing." The vital point is that you tell the truth. I have romanced many an item, but no telemarketer worth his order pad will tell an outright lie. This isn't based on a code of moral conduct as much as it is just good business sense.

USING THE VERNACULAR OF YOUR INDUSTRY

The three main assets one needs to be a successful telemarketer can be found in the three "Vs." Vernacular, vocabulary, and voice. If you speak the same language as the industry in which you are selling, you are ahead of the guy who does not have a clue as to what he is doing. To this end, product knowledge is vital. Bishop Sheen was asked how he could counsel couples with marital problems when he himself was never married. His reply was that one doesn't need to know how to build a car to drive one. It's the same way in sales. While it certainly is nice to understand the intricacies of the item you're selling, it's more important to understand its uses.

The question of credibility and the problem of vernacular work hand in hand. If we, as telemarketers, wish to be taken seriously by those we sell to, we must strive to know as much about what we sell as possible. When I sold electronics in the 1970s, I was overwhelmed with the amount of things I knew nothing about. Customers would ask me questions that I could not even begin to answer. Things such as SWR ratings, ohm capacity, and amp ratings left me in a state of electric confusion. I had no background in electronics. What I did have, however, was a talent for ferreting out the information my customer was seeking. The end result was I usually made the sale, but at times things looked doubtful.

Gradually, I learned the vernacular of the industry in which I was conducting business. Through much trial and error, I was able to finally enter a conversation with my customer and not sound like I just got off the boat. One way I overcame my lack of expertise in the electronics industry was to visit local electronics stores in my city. I learned the old-fashioned way—I asked questions. This technique will work in almost any industry and can be applied to any discipline.

Trade journals found at the corner magazine stand were also a major help to me. I even spent time in my local library, where I found a great deal of publications, books, and reference materials that filled the gaps in my education. There is no shame in not knowing an answer to a question. The shame comes from not looking for the answer. With increased knowledge came increased vernacular.

BE COGNIZANT OF YOUR VOCABULARY

As important as vernacular is, the second aspect of the three "Vs" is a real killer. Vocabulary. The words you use to describe a product are as important to the success of the sale as any of the features and benefits that the product possesses. Perhaps even more so. Words are to sales what colors are to painting. Each word, phrase, and sentence must be carefully chosen, not only to describe the product, but also to present it in the best light.

I mentioned the need to "romance" an item. Having sold almost every product that can be touted over a phone line, from cemetery plots and baby pictures to circus tickets and electronic hardware, the most important thing to discover was how to convince the person on the other end of the line that he wanted to buy what I had for sale. And want it bad enough to trade money for it.

This is the essence of selling. Having a product that someone else wants. Think about this. It is not as obvious as it sounds. Thomas has twenty dollars in his hand. Randy has a product in his. Thomas has managed through hard work to acquire the twenty dollars. Now comes Randy with a product that is obviously not as liquid as the cash Thomas has. The trick here is to influence Thomas to give over his money to Randy, take the possession from Randy's hand, and walk away—happy with the transaction! Thomas must have a song in his heart and a feeling that he's better off without the twenty dollars, with the newly acquired possession.

If you really stop to think this through, it is amazing that anyone ever buys anything. To conduct this entire transaction over the phone lines is even more amazing! After all, the person doing the buying can't even see what he's getting for his hard-earned cash.

Choose your words as carefully as an artist chooses his hues and shades. Be exact, yet be full of description. You are not selling pencils, you are selling precision writing instruments, constructed of the finest hardwoods and imported leads. You are not selling blenders. You are selling the most modern, time-saving device ever known to the American housewife, a device which will set her free to attend to more important aspects in her life. Think, people! Do you eat your chicken without salt? Do you buy only gray clothes and seek bland haircuts? Of course not! Why, then, would you attempt to sell a product without the enthusiasm and color which it so obviously deserves?

As a side note to the use of vocabulary, always take your lead from the person to whom you are speaking. *Never, I repeat, never use profanity while speaking on the phone to a customer!* Listen to his or her manner of expression. If the strongest thing the buyer says is, "Gosh, that makes me so darn mad . . .," then take your cue from that.

As I was preparing to go home one evening, my secretary put a call through to my office. She had mistaken a voice for that of someone else. It was not my friend, but rather a salesman. I sat back down at my desk. Out of professional courtesy, I decided to give him five minutes to make his pitch. Within the first minute of that call, the man managed to alienate me to the point I would not have bought five-dollar bills from him if they were a dollar apiece! And he'd done it all with his foul vocabulary.

I am not a plaster saint, and there have been times when people would have sworn I learned English from a one-eyed sailor, but this man had the foulest mouth I ever heard. To make matters worse, he didn't know anything at all about me. I found myself wondering what I had said to him that would give him the idea I would be tolerant of this foul verbiage. About three minutes into the call, he stopped his tirade of obscenities to say, "I hope my language doesn't offend you, but I'm the kind of guy who says what he thinks." I replied, "Then I better let you get off the phone, because I certainly would hate to be responsible for your continued need to think." With this I hung up and instructed my secretary never to put this man's call through again.

The point here is not that he used language I did not understand or had not heard before, but he presumed to use them without first finding out what type of person I was. As important as what we say is how we say it.

THE POWER OF VOICE

Vernacular and vocabulary are important. But I saved the best for last. Voice! Voice is one of the first things a police officer learns at the academy. When a cop tells you to step away from the car, you do so, not only because he has a badge and a gun, but also because he speaks with authority. It is the tone of voice that makes us shudder as we remember our father's deep bellows or our high school principal's firm timbre. Obviously, when we speak to our customers, we cannot intimidate them or attempt to inspire fear. We cannot order them to buy from us (oh, wouldst that we could!) and we cannot command them to pay attention. What we can do, however, is to speak with the voice of an informed and competent individual. We can, in a polite manner, retain control of the conversation and pilot that conversation down the road we wish them to follow.

Your voice is your suit of clothes, it is your shining shoes. It is your expensive watch, your flashy red sports car, and all the other accoutrements salesmen in the field use to gain the confidence of their customers. If your voice is weak, despondent, sad, hesitant, or in any way something other than sharp, crisp, clear, and aggressive, then you are beating yourself before the customer has a chance to hear you out. *Be positive!* Call with a voice of authority! Be sure of yourself, sure of your purpose. Try to keep in mind that while you have intruded on the peace and quiet of the buyer's day, you are also calling for a reason. You are calling to help him buy your product.

That's right! *You are calling to help.* If you approach sales in general with a mealy attitude, one which portrays you as weak and indecisive, do you really think anyone is going to listen to what you have to say, much less act on your suggestions? Of course not! I'm not suggesting that you need to be a bully. I'm saying that you need to portray an attitude of professionalism and maintain the posture of a positive, confident salesperson.

IN PARTING . . .

You would have no faith in a doctor who sat in front of you wringing his hands and stuttering while searching for the right thing to do. You would probably get off any airplane on which you heard the pilot confiding to the stewardess that there sure were a lot of buttons and switches in the cockpit. Selling is no different. No one, not a single person you will meet as you practice and perfect your art, will want to buy from a person who seems like an incompetent amateur. Voice—the ability to put your message across with the proper amount of honesty and expertise—will win the day. Your ability to orchestrate and present to the buyer a concise, accurate, and reasonably positive mental picture of what you can do for him will depend in large part on how well your voice can carry your presence.

eleven

Overcoming Specific Objections

I mentioned earlier in this book I would address specific objections as they are likely to be presented to the telemarketer and provide specific remedies to those objections. While it would be an impossible task to name them all, the next few pages should prove helpful as you delicately tiptoe across the minefield of the dreaded objection.

IT COSTS TOO MUCH

"Too much" is a three-sided sword in telemarketing. The first is the obvious one, "it costs too much." As I have stated earlier, cost is perhaps the least problematic of all objections. There is a definite distinction between the terms *cost* and *value.* If you compare the price of a new luxury sedan over the price of a fifteen-year-old jalopy, the difference is startling. But if you consider the value of both automobiles, the difference suddenly becomes justified.

With rare exceptions, no two telemarketers are selling the exact same product. If the product you are selling has a somewhat higher price point than a similar product sold by a competitor, overcome the price difference by stressing the ways in which your product is superior. Don't overlook any possibility. Package design, color, quantity in package, number of packages in inner carton, number of inner cartons in master carton, availability of the product, warranty, and serviceability of the item are all intangible qualities that may give your product an edge over your competition.

Always compare apples to apples when your competition has a similar product at a lower price. No one consistently sells at a loss. If Company A is selling its products at a substantially lower price than Company B, one of three factors is at work. First, Company A is buying cheaper products, thus offering an inferior item. If this is the case, you have nothing to fear provided you are salesman enough to skillfully point out the obvious. Inferior products invariably result in customer dissatisfaction.

Second, Company A is selling its products cheaper because they have a temporary markdown of an item or a group of items. These temporary markdowns or sale items are not a reflection of overall lower prices but rather are intended to move certain items quickly, perhaps to make room for newer models, perhaps to clear dead merchandise out of stock, perhaps in anticipation of discontinuing a product line. *Don't panic!* Your company does the same thing when it runs a promotion.

Last, Company A may be in financial difficulties, thereby creating an environment which requires a drastic cut in prices to insure a sustained cash flow. This dagger cuts both ways, however, for in addition to cutting prices, they are also cutting profits. Cutting profits will result in a tightening of cash flow, not an influx of capital. The first rush of business may seem like the answer to a cash-starved company, but ultimately, reliance on sales and promotions will result in certain ruination.

Do not be intimidated by lower prices! Do not put your head in the sand and pretend there is nothing you can do. Fight back! Find the chink in your competitor's pricing and attack. Ask questions. Find out if the competition's terms are as liberal as those offered by your firm. What about freight? Warranty? Get to the meat of the issue. How long has your competition been in business? Are they liable to still be in business a year from now when problems may begin to develop with the merchandise they are selling today?

A gas station located a few blocks from my home put up a huge sign in front of its building. It simply read:

OUR GAS CONTAINS NO WATER!

I asked the owner what the sign meant. He explained that it meant just what it said. I asked him if the station across the street sold gas containing water. He replied, "I don't know. All I know is that my gas doesn't!"

He wasn't making grand claims that his petroleum was any better than the guy's across the street, nor was he saying his competition was selling substandard products. He was simply allowing a statement of fact to plant a seed of doubt in the consumer brain. By employing a billboard to announce that his gas was free of water, he was in effect laying the burden of guilt on his competitor to make a similar statement. If he did not, it could be assumed that the gas across the street was indeed contaminated by water. And all this was done without slander or accusation. The implications are obvious.

TOO MUCH PRODUCT

The second use of "too much" as an objection regards quantity. If you have pitched a deal to someone and they respond by saying, "That's a good deal, but I couldn't begin to use that much product," what he is saying is really, "Yeah, I'd buy that, but there's too much of it." There is a solution to this. The object is to minimize the amount of product and at the same time maximize the potential for profit.

While working for a telemarketing automotive supply company, I ran a promotion on valve stems for tires. The deal consisted of 1,000 stems packed in a plastic box at half the regular price. This required an investment of about $100 and, of course, resulted in a savings to the customer of a like amount. In short, he would be receiving $200 worth of product for half the price.

Now, 1,000 valve stems is a lot of stems. The first thing most of my customers said was, "I won't sell 1,000 of those things in two years." They said this because they were in the habit of buying stems in quantities of 200 at a time. The first thing I had to do was overcome their resistance. I did this by pointing out the obvious. First, I broke the deal down by saying, "Look, you sell four stems every time you sell a set of tires, so really, we're only talking about 250 sales here. Secondly, when you normally buy these from me, you buy them a couple hundred at a time, and you place an order at least once a month. I know we're talking about a three- or four-month supply, but they're only costing you half price. So, in reality, you're really only buying a few hundred more than you would normally purchase anyway. After you've sold the first 250 stems, you're ahead of the game."

Having broke down the deal in such a manner, the objection to cost was gone. I was still left with the problem of storage, inventory control, and freight. Freight was easily dealt with. In fact, I was able to use it as a selling point. It cost less to receive one shipment of 1,000 pieces than five shipments of 200 pieces. In regard to inventory control, larger deliveries actually cut down on the paperwork involved in maintaining an ongoing inventory system.

The only sticky problem with this deal was storage. It did indeed require five times the storage space to shelve

1,000 stems than it did to shelve 200. I pointed out, however, that these are small items to begin with and surely the outstanding savings incorporated into this deal made the temporary inconvenience of storage a minor problem.

If I had allowed the quantity of items to remain in my buyer's mind as a huge mountain of product, chances are I would never have sold any of the deals. As it turned out, we moved a record number of stems that month. I was successful, not because I am a supersalesman or because the product was in hot demand, but rather because the customer was made to see the possibilities the deal offered.

TOO MUCH INVENTORY

The third "too much" stems from existing inventory. When a customer says he has "too much" of a similar item already in inventory and you are trying to sell him still more of the same type of product, a different approach is needed. Let's set up a scenario.

It's August. The customer is a retail drugstore, and you're selling notebook paper. Your customer tells you he already has an overabundance of paper. In fact, he has paper left over from the last school term.

Determine how much paper he has in inventory. He tells you he has 200 packages left in stock. Your objective should not be to try to sell him more to add to an already overstocked situation. What you need is a way to make the 200 packages seem like insufficient stock. How? What about an in-store promotion? What if your customer were to build a huge wall of notebook paper and run it on sale at 20 percent off its regular price? After all, it is August. School starts in a few weeks. What better time to run a promotion on school supplies? At 20 percent off, the store will still turn a profit, and the sale will create additional traffic into the store, traffic which will result in additional sales of pencils, notebook binders, rulers, markers and other school-related items.

The problem is, with only 200 packages of paper, he really can't build much of a display. He'll definitely need to order more product from you.

Do you see what we've done here? With 200 packages of notebook paper, your customer was overstocked for his shelves. But, for a giant display, he was at least 1,000 packages short. We have taken a product your customer assumed was overstocked and shown it to be insufficient. As a result, he will increase his business, create more walk-in traffic, and ultimately earn the goodwill of his customers for providing an item on sale at a time when it was most in demand, i.e., the reopening of school.

These approaches to the objection of "too much" will not only result in increased sales but will separate you from the order takers. It is not so much a question of being glib as it is an opportunity for you to shine. We are talking about the question of perception. Until the solutions for the problems of "too much" were employed, your opportunities for additional sales were limited, not by your limitations, but rather by the limitations imposed upon you by the buyer. With skill and foresight you can overcome the objection of "too much." Anyone can take an order. Only a creative salesperson can develop a market where none existed before!

NOT ENOUGH NEED, TIME, OR MONEY

While "too much" can be a broad tent for the customer to hide under, it's nothing compared to "not enough." "Not enough" covers a lot of ground. Primarily, however, it is an excuse used by buyers when they really don't want to commit to a particular order, yet they want to keep you on a back burner in case they should need you in an emergency.

No Need

One version of "not enough" is when the buyer continually tells you he will be ready to buy shortly, but right now he just doesn't have enough of an order to make it worth your while. This type of customer is one of the most frustrating. He is perennially "on the verge" but never quite ready to commit. What to do? First, make sure he is really the buyer. It may well be that the individual you are calling is, in reality, not the person who makes the decisions. Few things are more difficult than trying to sell a product through a middle party. Your best attempts at salesmanship may be lost in translation. It is akin to wearing a raincoat while taking a shower.

If, after you have repeatedly tried to get a commitment out of a buyer, he still remains a blushing bride, drastic measures are in order. You must move him to action. When faced with this kind of situation, I use a two-step process. First, I listen while the buyer dances around the order pad, telling me there are things he needs, but right now there just isn't enough to justify an order. After he has committed himself as far as he will, I tell him that if he'd like, I'll start to write an order, but not process it until he's got enough for a shipment. This will sometimes move him toward a decision.

In selling, every order has to start somewhere. If you can get the buyer to commit to one item at least, you have a fighting chance to finish the order. Until he does, however, you will merely provide your ulcer with more fodder. Get him to agree that you've got the best price he has ever seen on glow-in-the-dark toothpicks. Get him to agree that he will be the first merchant to have such an item in stock; then, ask for the order. When he says to you, "I really hate to order just toothpicks," you reply, "I understand. Why don't I just make a note of your interest in them, and when we have enough of an order to justify shipping, I'll get them out to you?"

Get your prospect to agree that he eventually will order three gross of this item. Write it up. Now mind you, I didn't say ship it, only write it up. Now, find another item he likes. Perhaps the nuclear-powered toothbrush shaped like Shammu the Killer Whale. Great! How many would he like? I know, I know, not enough to order—but how many? Six dozen? Wonderful! Write it up. See the pattern? Coax and gently lead this man down the yellow brick road of sales. Guide him gently. After he's found four or five items and, after you have calculated the total amount of the order, gently inform him that miracle of miracles, he has sufficient products ordered to justify ship-ment. Get a purchase order number, go over the order with him and tell him good bye.

The problem here is the man wanted to buy all along, only he was afraid to look like small potatoes. He was withholding his business for fear you would think him a small customer. He was hesitant to place an order, not be-cause he is a heavy hitter, used to big buys, but quite the opposite. He was afraid you would think less of him. He was afraid you would not respect him.

Not Enough Time

"Not enough" can take other forms even more insidious. A buyer can have "not enough" time to talk to you. There was a buyer I pursued for two weeks. Every time I called, he was too busy to talk. Now, this happens, but not all the time. Every time I called he would suddenly develop a cri-sis that would pull him away from the phone as soon as he heard my voice. I would be told, "Call back later."

Later never came. Finally, one afternoon I got through to him. His first words to me, after I identified myself were, "Can't talk. Call me later." I responded with only one word. "No." After five seconds of silence, he spoke.

"What?"

"No. I've called you fifteen times in two weeks, and each time I call you tell me to call you back later. I understand you're a busy man, but your actions now border on being rude."

Understand this. I was not trying to save this sale. I had reached the point where I no longer thought this man was ever going to be a viable customer, and I just wanted the satisfaction of telling him what I thought. I'd like to tell you he apologized and we went on to establish a long and friendly relationship, but it did not work out that way. He slammed the phone in my ear.

A week later I called him back. Obviously, he and I had gotten off to a bad start, and if he were willing to listen to what I had to sell, I would be willing to be more understanding of the time restraints he was working within. Finally something worked. He was a customer of mine for seven years.

Not Enough Money

Of all the "not enoughs," not enough money is a real killer. Customers have told me they were out of money and couldn't pay their bills let alone buy a new line of merchandise. There is a standard reply I use for this. I tell them I don't want to sell them my whole warehouse, only a tiny, little part of it. I add that if they are short of funds, the only way a retail operation has to raise cash is through sales. And without merchandise, they've got nothing to sell. You can't sell from an empty wagon! Show your customer that the best means he has to raise cash is to buy merchandise from you, sell it, and bank the profits.

Your customer may tell you he hasn't had enough interest in a certain item or he has never sold a particular item. This is not a valid reason to cease trying to sell the new product. I've had them tell me, "No one ever asked me for a life-size poster of Attila the Hun." I have a standard reply: no one asked Henry Ford for a Model T until he started producing them. Appeal to the adventurer in your buyer. My favorite phrase when introducing a new product to a customer is, "I'm not saying you should mortgage the farm to buy all I have. I'm just suggesting that you try a few of these."

It is incumbent on us, as the visionaries of the business future, to introduce new items and new concepts. I have found the phrase, "I'm not trying to sell you these just to make a sale," very effective. Obviously, I was trying to make a sale, but just as obviously, I was looking at future business that would result from the acceptance of any new line or item. It is often the new item that allows us to get our foot in the door.

With established customers I often rely on the introduction of new items to begin my sales call. I will start a great number of calls with statements like, "Have I got a great new item for you," or, "I've just been given a new item that's really going to be hot!" This approach piques the interest of the customer and at the same time allows the new product to lead into regular line items.

As with the objection of "too much," the objection of "not enough" can be defeated in all its many forms. The real test of a telemarketer's skills lies not in his or her ability to push merchandise, but rather in his or her ability to solve problems. *The buyer's job is to buy. Your job is to sell.* All that stands between you and the performance of your duties are a few minor problems—objections if you will. Solve the problem and make the sale.

IT'S TOO EARLY

The objection of "too early" is frequently heard in telemarketing. It is particularly a bane of seasonal goods. Goods such as Christmas cards, Easter bunnies, valentine hearts, and so on fit this category. "Too early," in these cases, can be a valid objection. There are two ways to combat this. The first is with economic incentives; the other is with fear tactics.

Economic incentives must be true incentives if they are to be perceived as such. They can take the form of early-bird discounts, free freight, delayed billings, or in some cases, co-op advertising. Displays, window posters, and other point-of-purchase items will also be perceived as justifications for buying 100 dozen pairs of beach sandals in the dead of winter. There are three very good reasons to push your customer into an early purchase of seasonal items.

The first is, obviously, to earn a commission. The second and less tangible reason is that by filling your customer's warehouse with all the ice skates he can possibly store in the early part of April, you deny your competitor accessibility to that customer in September when he would normally be placing his orders for ice skates. The third advantage is that by moving the merchandise from your warehouse to his, you will have created an influx of dollars in the bank and space in your warehouse, both of which can be put to better use than the storage of an item which will not begin to sell for another six months.

The second way to overcome the "too early" objection is to panic the buyer into an early purchase based on the oldest of emotions: greed. While I was in the electronics industry, it became obvious that every Christmas a shortage of nickel-cadmium batteries would occur. This was, of course, caused by the excessive number of items requiring this type of battery. These items would sell in large numbers each year for Christmas presents. Because of the cost of Ni-Cad batteries, most dealers would wait until the last minute and then try to purchase them wherever they could.

One year, in June, I decided to turn this shortage to my advantage. I sent out a sale flier and followed it with a phone campaign. The thrust of the flier was a picture of Old Saint Nick walking away from his sled with an obviously empty bag. The caption read: "Sorry, kids, but I ran out of Ni-Cads *again* this year!" This was followed in large, bold type with: "Don't Get Caught Short! Order Ni-Cads Now!" The result? For the first time in the history of our company, we sold completely out of Ni-Cad batteries in the month of June! And, the sales continued through July and August also.

IT'S TOO LATE

The "too late" objection is really an extension of the "too early" objection. When is an item too late? It is only too late when the retailer can no longer sell the item due to a lack of interest or need for the product. One of the distributors I represented a few years ago had an incredibly high inventory of electronic toys. The Christmas season had come and gone, and still the product sat on his shelves. His first inclination was to mark them down and clear them out. I suggested to him, however, that if they would appeal to buyers because of price, they should also appeal because of scarcity. I reasoned that if everyone had unloaded their inventory of remote controlled cars during the peak selling season, it stood to reason that after Christmas there might have been a shortage of these items. I called several dealers, all of which had ordered these cars during the regular selling season, and asked how they had fared with the toys. To the man, they all said the items had sold well and that they were satisfied with the response they received.

Each dealer added that he could have sold several dozen more if he had had them in stock in time to sell. Why not, I asked, stock them all year long. The standard reply I received was that Christmas comes but once a year. True, but so do birthdays, graduations, hospital stays, and other events for which people purchase gifts. The end result? I was able to sell the remaining inventory at full price in the weeks following Christmas. There is life after December, and many of my dealers were able to see the possibilities of carrying this line all year round.

IN PARTING ...

It is very difficult to create an artificial shortage or stage a panic—something I would never recommend. What I do recommend is a realistic assessment of the hard economic facts of life. First come, first serve. Make your customer understand that the realities of business call for him to be forever prepared for any eventuality, for any increase in sales, for any downward trend in production. The dangers of buying too early are far outweighed by the dangers of not buying at all.

Epilogue

This is a new age, an age of immediate response to immediate problems. I wrote this book for a multitude of reasons. The obvious ones were financial and ego-related. The real one is the fact that I believe in telemarketing. I believe it is a good and noble undertaking, and I believe it will feed other families as it has mine.

Everything I have written here is the truth, and everything here will help make you the superstar you can be. There's more I'd like to tell you, but my phone is ringing!

Good luck!

ABOUT THE AUTHOR

Phillip E. Mahfood owned and operated a telemarketing sales company for over twenty years. He is now a consultant specializing in the establishment and management of telecommuting and telemarketing divisions. Mr. Mahfood writes a syndicated editorial column and hosts his own radio talk show, syndicated from Tyler, Texas. A frequent guest speaker, he travels extensively to conduct seminars on telemarketing and telecommuting. Mr. Mahfood is the author of *Home Work: How to Hire, Manage & Monitor Employees Who Work at Home* (Probus, 1992). He resides in Tyler, Texas, with his wife, Karen.